Vintage Dreams Of The Sea

GRAYSCALE ART
COLORING BOOK

By Cheryl Korotky

The World of Enchanted Imagination

Hello Fellow Colorist

Welcome to

"The World of Enchanted Imagination" by Cheryl Korotky.

When I was a little girl I used to watch my grandmother color enhancing old B&W family photos. The work Nana produced was beautiful! She loved adding colorful life to otherwise, drab and badly faded memories. She used a variety of mediums, including colored pencils, watercolor and even crayons. When Nana was finished, she would frame the print and proudly display her new trophy for all to admire.

It was these cherished memories from my childhood, as well as the growing adult coloring trend that gave me the idea of producing high-quality, grayscale picture/coloring books. These will probably differ from what you are accustom to working with. I want to offer people the opportunity to produce genuine works of art; pictures of "REAL" animals, people, nature, etc. as well as Fantasy!

Grayscale is like a guide to help you along. You simply follow the natural shading. Completed projects are breathtaking, although there sometimes may be a learning curve like with any new skill, but practice makes perfect! There are some people who ONLY color grayscale! I hope you will become one of them. I occasionally see negative reviews on my fellow grayscale authors' pages mentioning the pictures were just regular photos made B&W. Well, exactly! That's what grayscale is!

Please join my Enchanted Imagination Grayscale Coloring Group at:

https://www.facebook.com/groups/1296319000437408/

Together we can grow and help each other with positive encouragement. This is the page where you can share your completed work from The World of Enchanted Imagination coloring books. Looking forward to seeing you there...

HAPPY COLORING!

BASIC INSTRUCTIONS

This book is produced though KDP, which means the paper will be of medium weight and good for colored pencils. That being said, I ask you to please follow some simple and basic instructions to help you enjoy your coloring experience.

If possible, watch some grayscale tutorials online. It will make a difference. The education is invaluable and there are so many exceptional coloring artists that can help guide your journey to achieve beautiful pictures. As you continue to color, the more grayscale you do, the better your pictures will become. Be aware, for most people there is definitely a learning curve when first discovering grayscale but the end results are worth it.

Try choosing about 3 or more colors in the same hue for each section you are working on. Follow along the naturally occurring shadows of the grayscale. Have some scrap paper (in back of book) next to you so you can try the colors you are using and how well they blend and complement each other. Colored pencils do not erase well (some not at all) so it's better to discover that the two greens don't blend well together on scrap paper instead of on your artwork.

Always put at least a piece of paper but best to use cardstock or cardboard between your pages as you are working. This will help prevent bleed-through as well as pressure transfer to the other pictures. You may also cut the pictures out with an exacto knife or scissors. If you prefer using a wet medium I suggest copying on an alternative, high quality paper because the book's paper probably won't be able to accommodate anything that can be readily absorbed. I do allow copies as long as for your own personal use and that's even a great idea for practicing. Colored pencils are fine, even with blending.

Great coloring art is created by using several layers of color and blending. Start out light and keep adding more colors & layers. Different pressure levels are also helpful. Keep trying different mediums to discover what you like. My personal favorites are colored pencils, watercolor pencils and gel pens. Color, brings your artwork to LIFE!

Watch for a downloadable version of this book as well as a pocket-size. This is a 3-part series. Watch for Let's Get Married and Let's Have a Baby!

Don't forget to join my coloring group. I can't wait to see your completed work!

https://www.facebook.com/groups/2392264234228891/

Practice! Practice! Practice!

The more grayscale you do, the better your results will be.

Cheryl Korotky grew up in Port Jervis, NY and received her very first camera at the age of 10. She started taking pictures of family, friends and the family cat and has been hooked ever since. Now a professional, multi-award winning photographer and proprietor of **A Heartbeat in Time Photography**, her specialties include child photography and B&W/grayscale.

Discover her work at:

https://www.facebook.com/AHeartbeatInTimePhotography

Also on Pixoto where you can see her awards for **Top Photographer of the Year** in **Babies & Children** and **B&W**:

http://www.pixoto.com/cheryl.korotky/recent

Come join our coloring group, The World of Enchanted Imagination Coloring where we encourage you to share & celebrate your completed artwork from our books.

When Cheryl is not taking pictures (her family affectionately calls her, "The Paparazzi"), you can find her exercising, gardening, cooking, teaching, reading, writing, painting or coloring. An avid nature-lover, she makes her home in the mountains of NE Pennsylvania (Equinunk) with her family and various pets and wildlife.

She is currently working on several grayscale coloring books for **The World of Enchanted Imagination,** many now already in print. Also, she will be publishing a group of children's books from **The Stories Your Child Will Actually Want to Read** series as well as several novels in the works. Watch for her upcoming books.

This book is dedicated to my grandmother, Gladys Wickham, who taught me the joy of seeing the world in color. Also, to my entire family and daughters, Tracy Dupre, Chelsea Wells, as well as my 4 grandchildren, Nevaeh & Peyton Wells, Adam Dupre & Grayson Kramer.
And last but not least, to my fiance, Frederick Peckham, who always believes in me and all my endeavors.

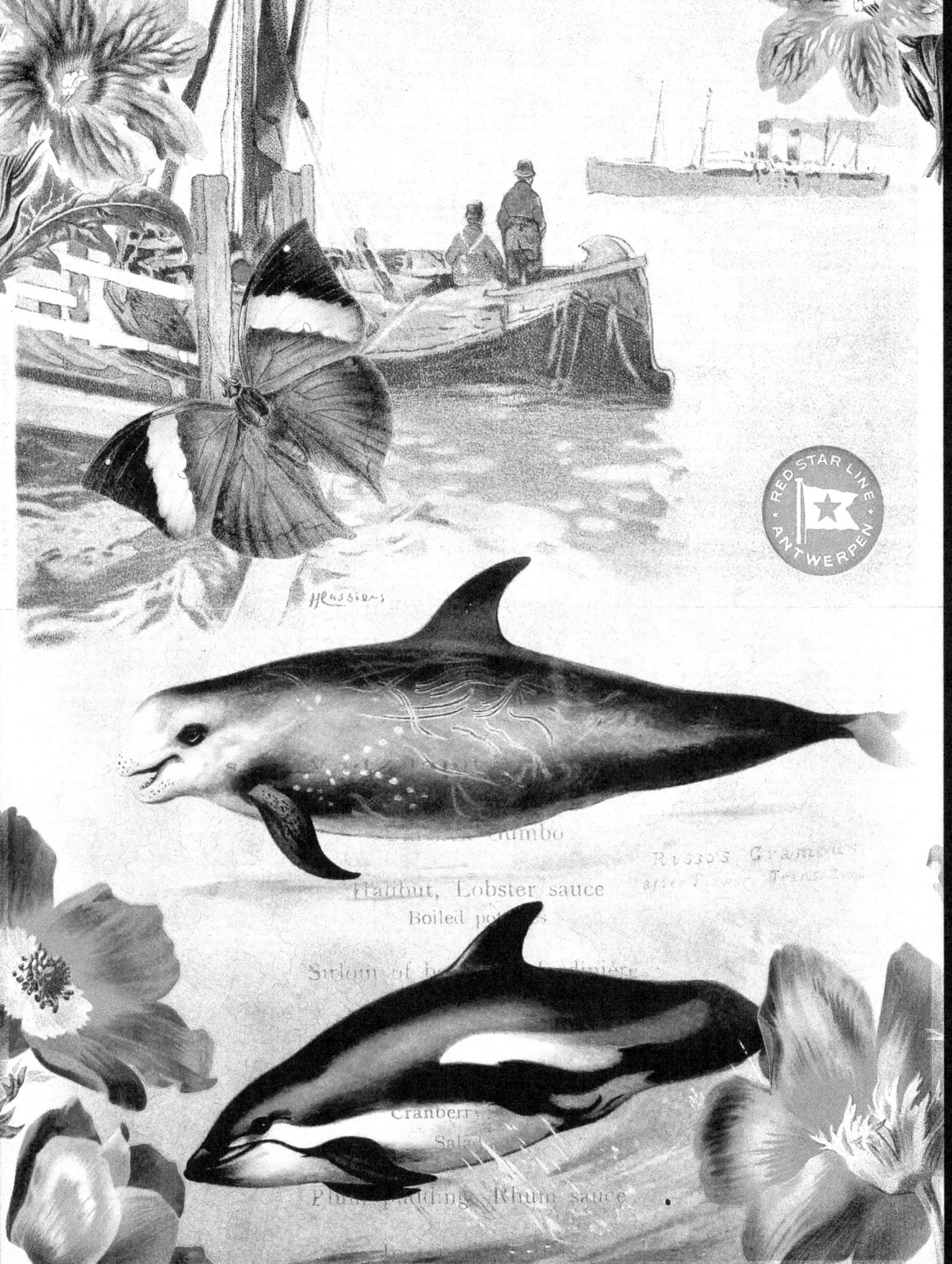

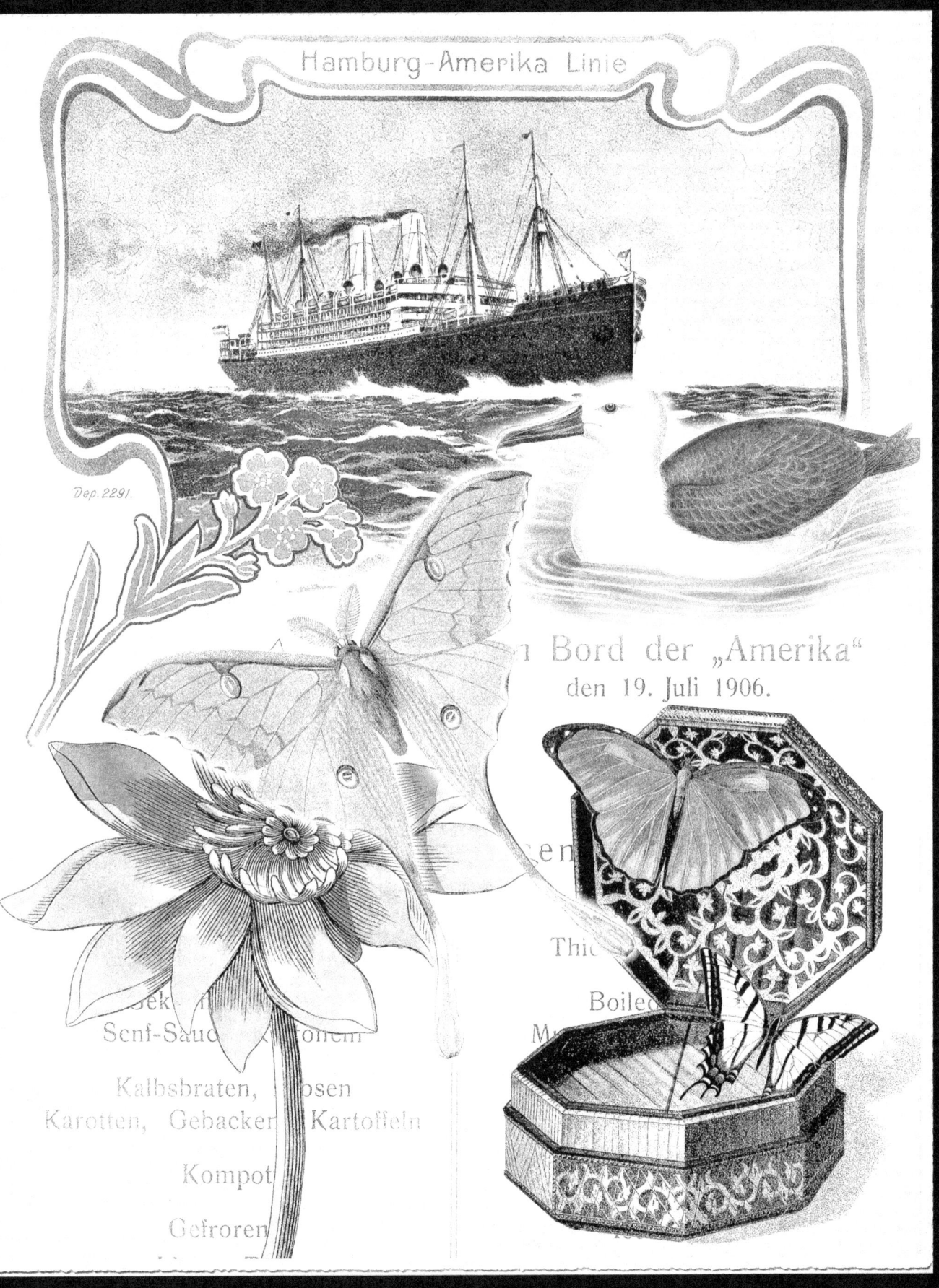

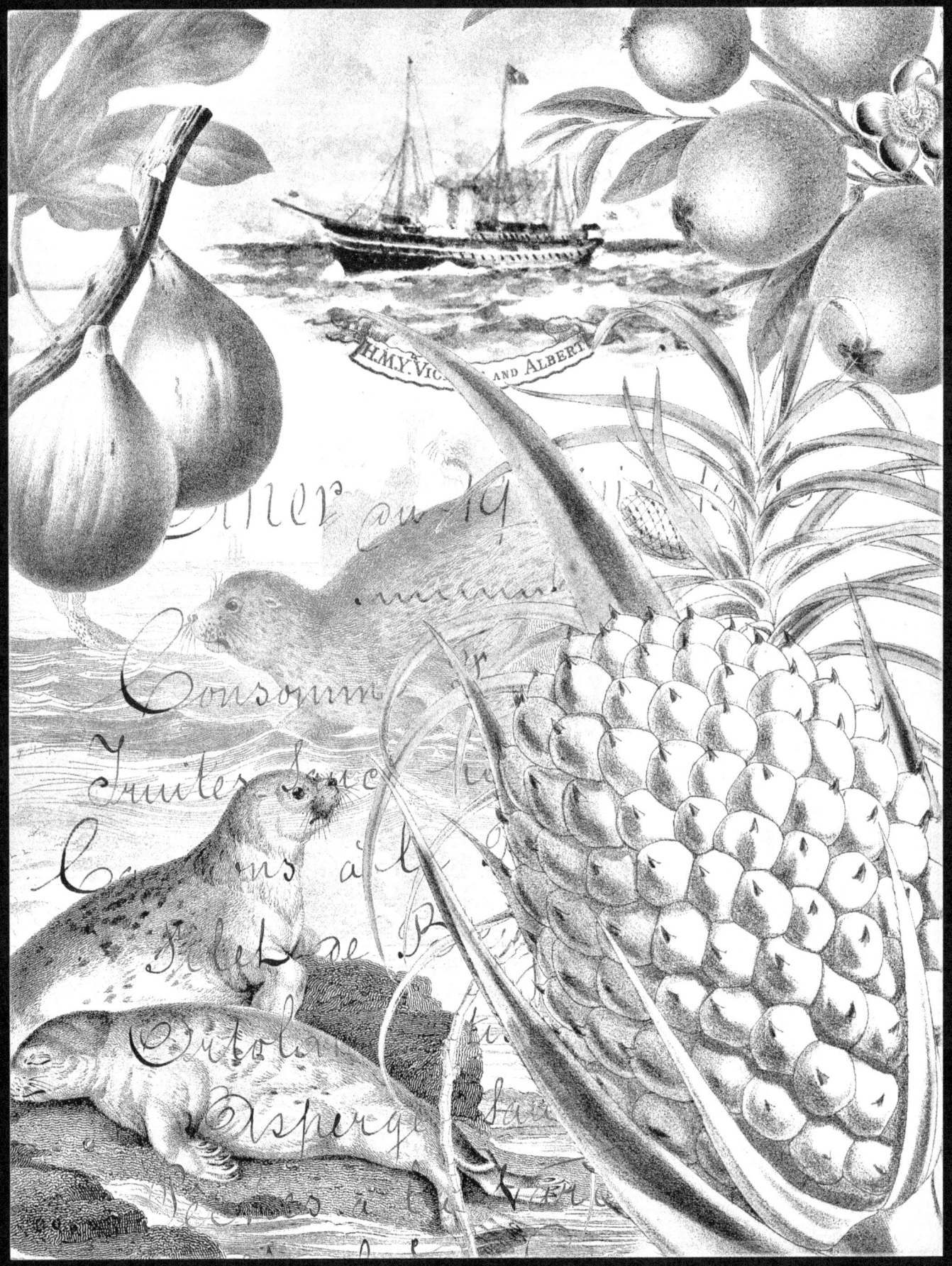

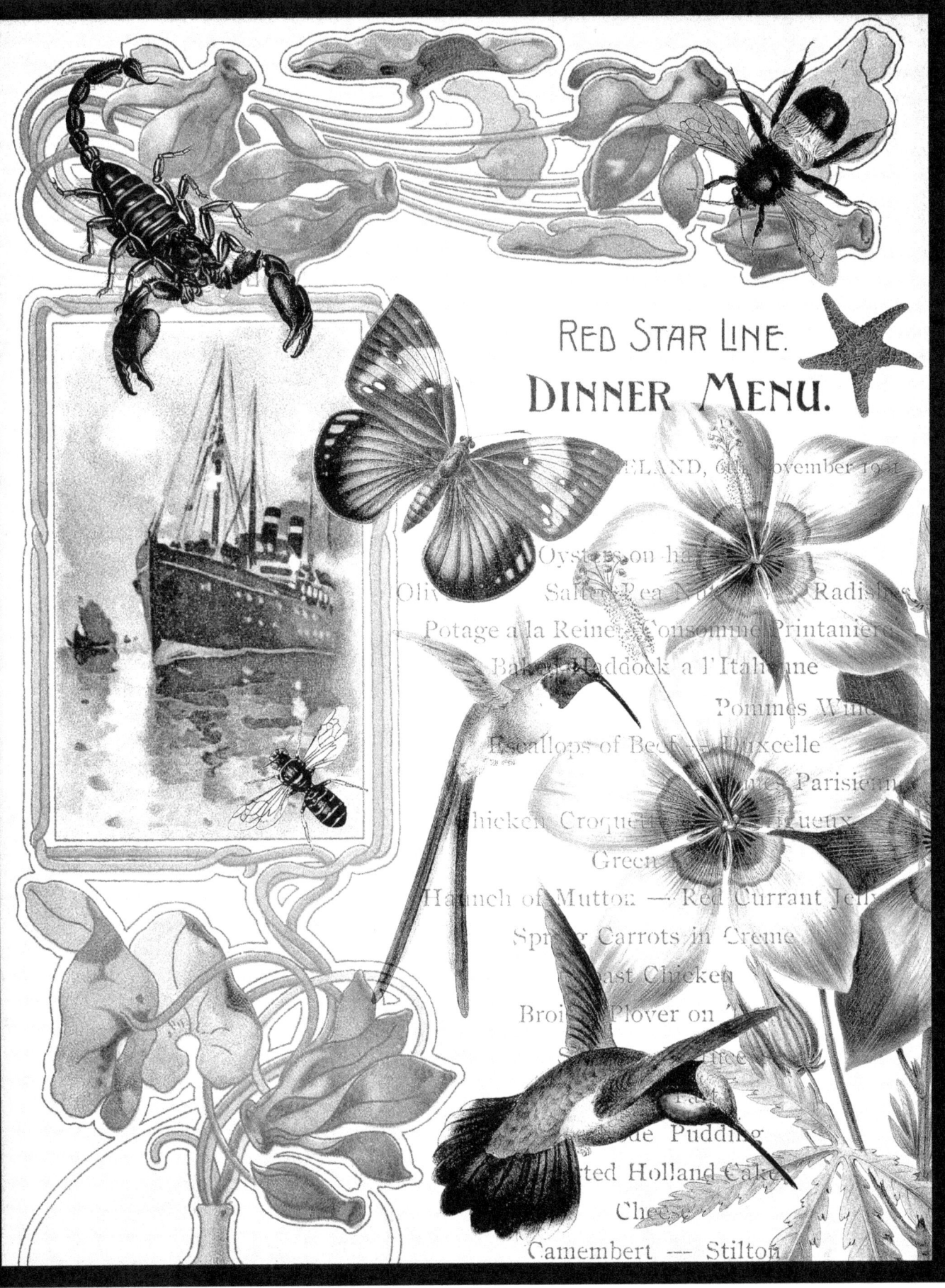

Red Star Line.
Dinner Menu.

ZEELAND, 6th November 1901

Oysters on half shell
Olives --- Salted Pea Nuts --- Radishes
Potage a la Reine --- Consommé Printanière
Baked Haddock a l'Italienne
Pommes Wine
Escallops of Beef --- Duxcelle
Parisienne
Chicken Croquettes --- Rigueux
Greens
Haunch of Mutton --- Red Currant Jelly
Spring Carrots in Creme
Roast Chicken
Broiled Plover on Toast
Salad --- Lettuce
Pudding
Assorted Holland Cakes
Cheese
Camembert --- Stilton

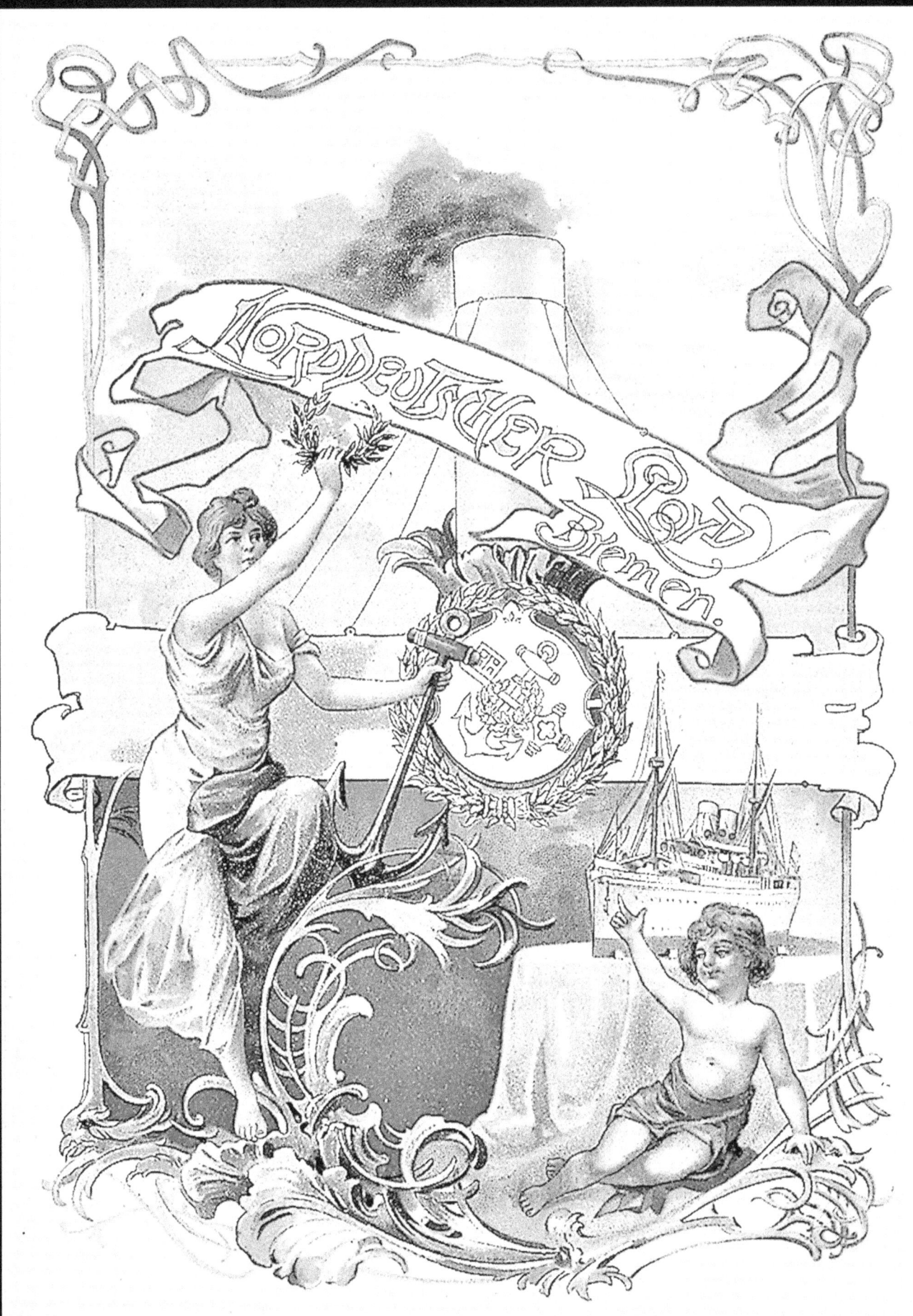

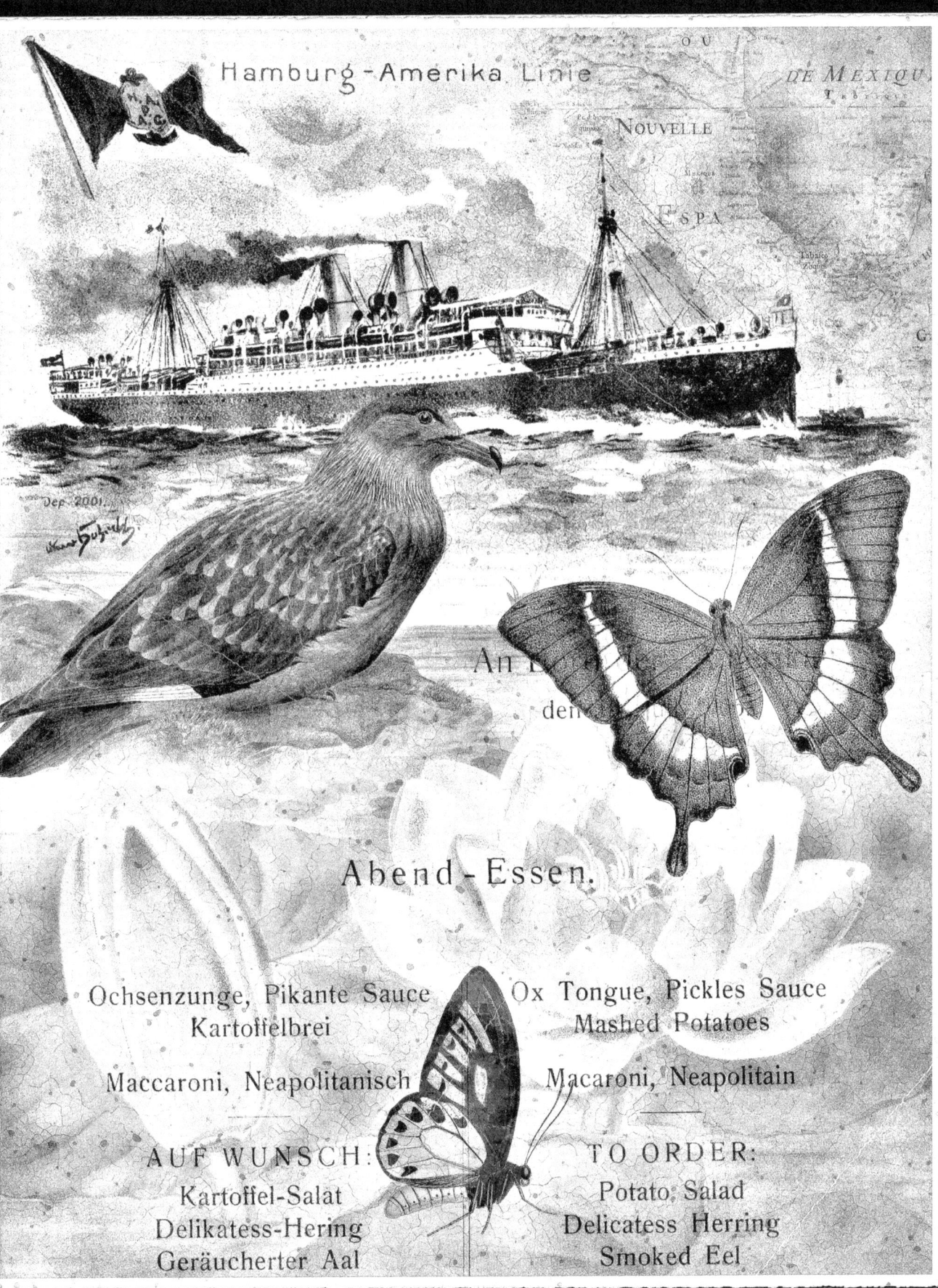

Hamburg-Amerika Linie

Abend-Essen.

Ochsenzunge, Pikante Sauce	Ox Tongue, Pickles Sauce
Kartoffelbrei	Mashed Potatoes
Maccaroni, Neapolitanisch	Macaroni, Neapolitain

AUF WUNSCH:	TO ORDER:
Kartoffel-Salat	Potato Salad
Delikatess-Hering	Delicatess Herring
Geräucherter Aal	Smoked Eel

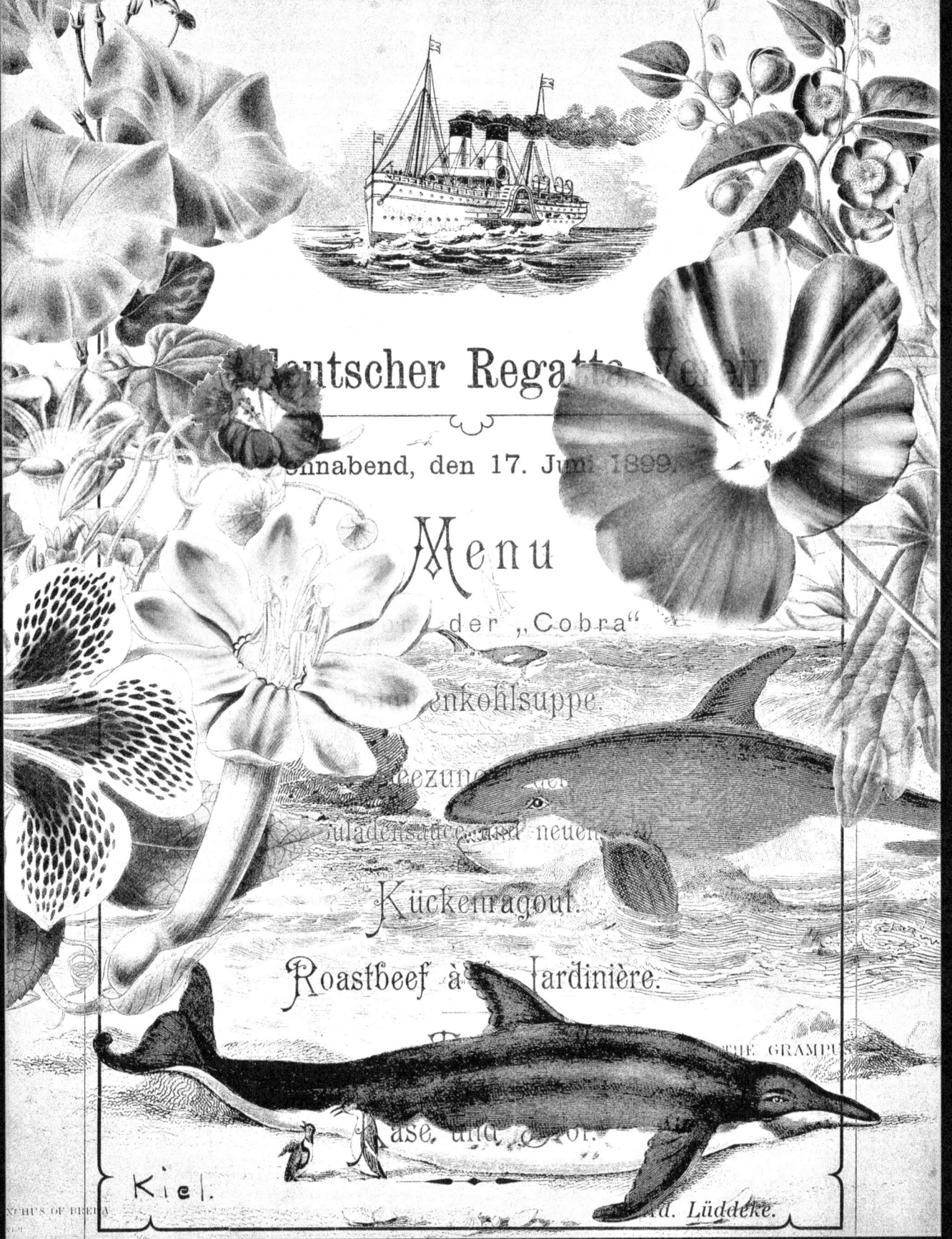

Deutscher Regatta-Verein

Sonnabend, den 17. Juni 1899

Menu

der „Cobra"

...enkohlsuppe.

...eezunge...

...uladensauce...und neuen...

Kückenragout.

Roastbeef à la Jardinière.

...äse und...

Kiel.   Ad. Lüddeke.

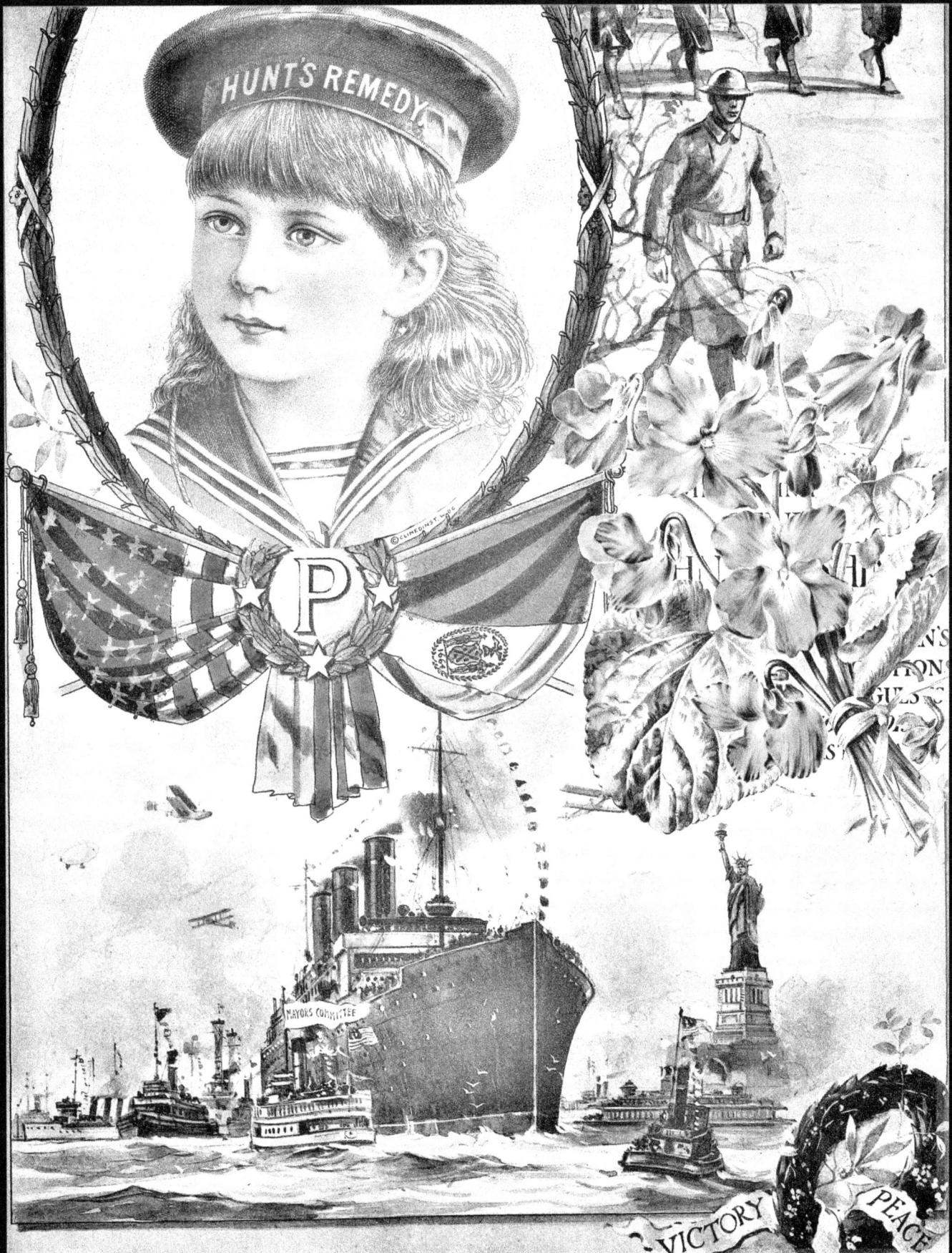

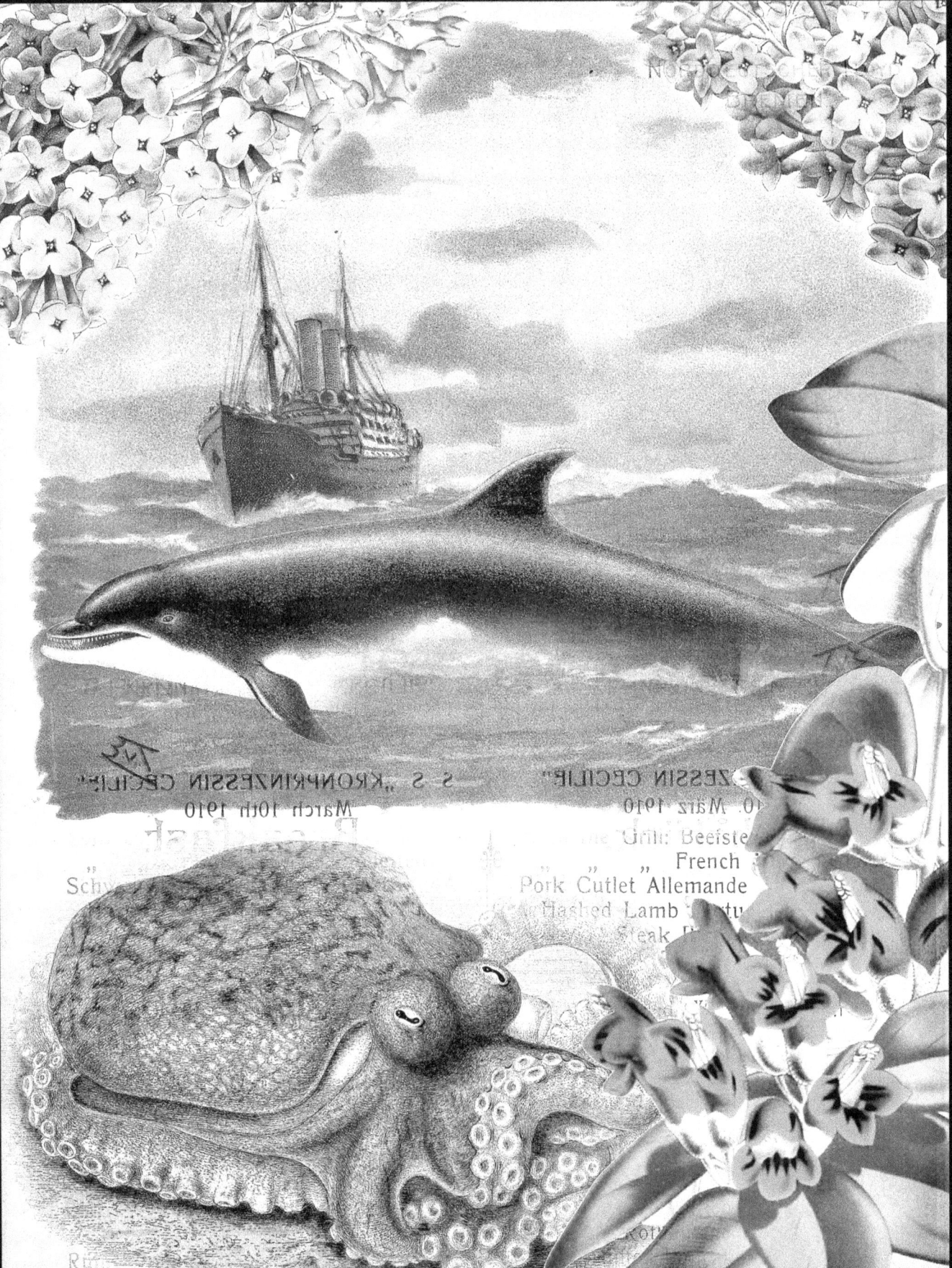

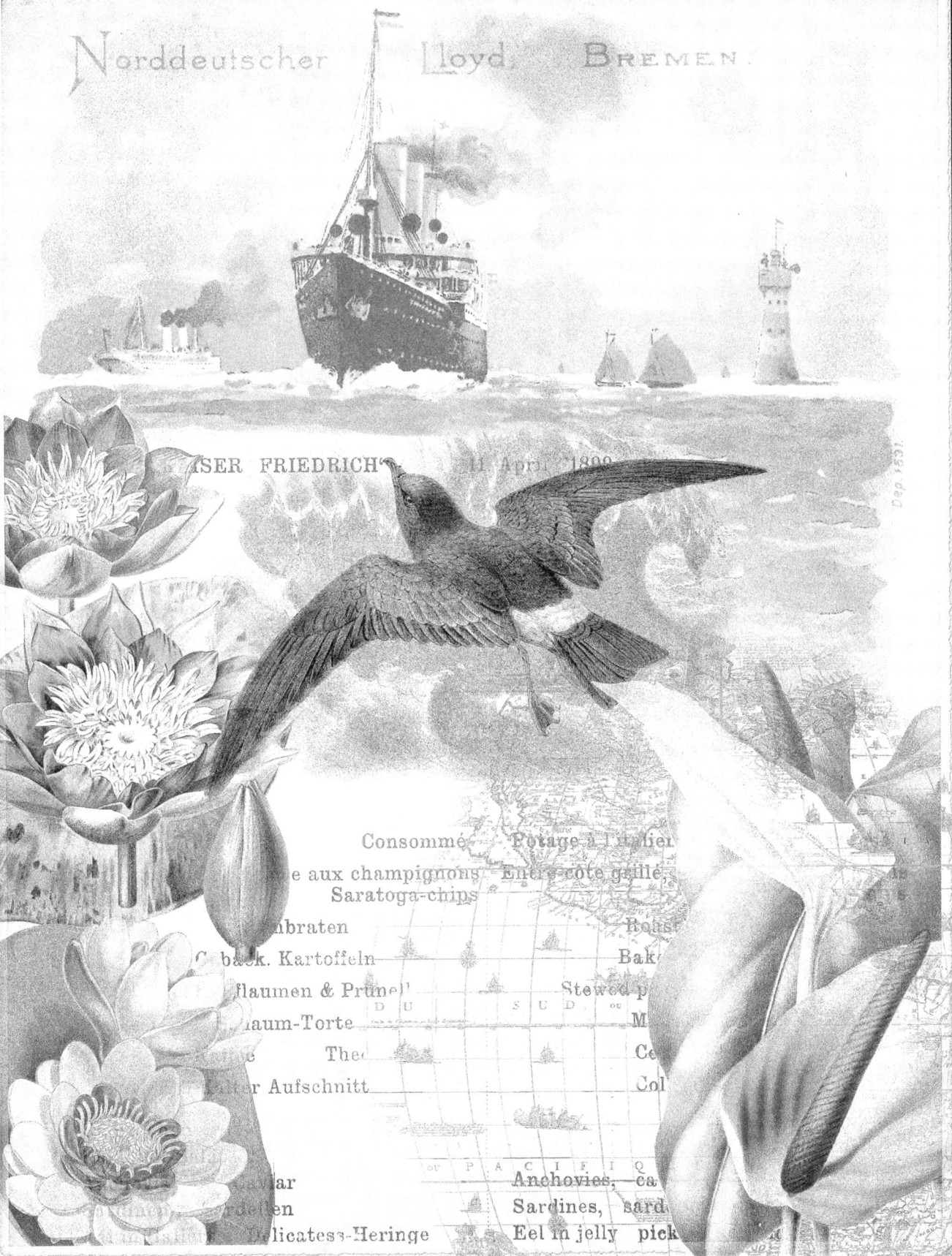

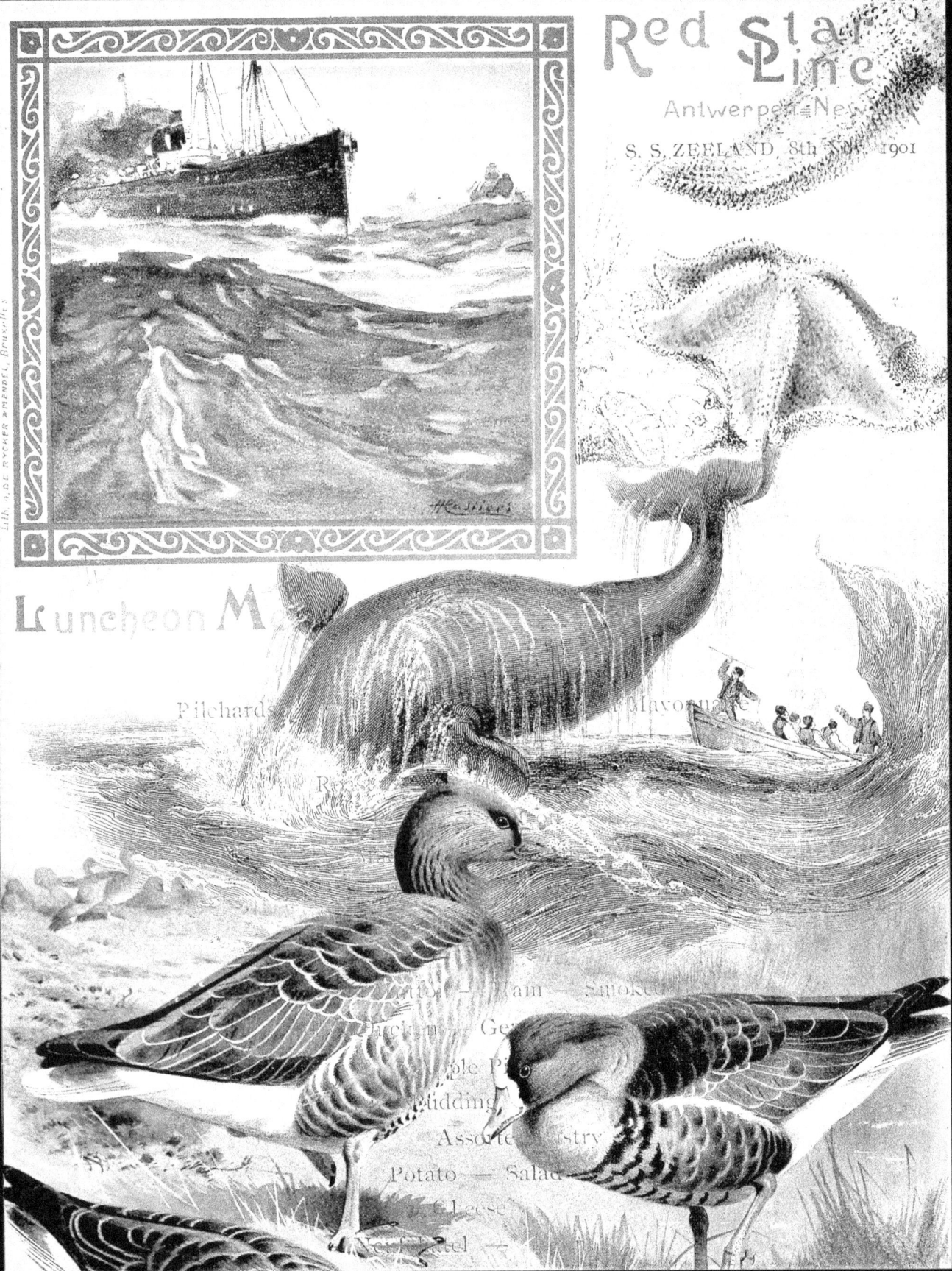

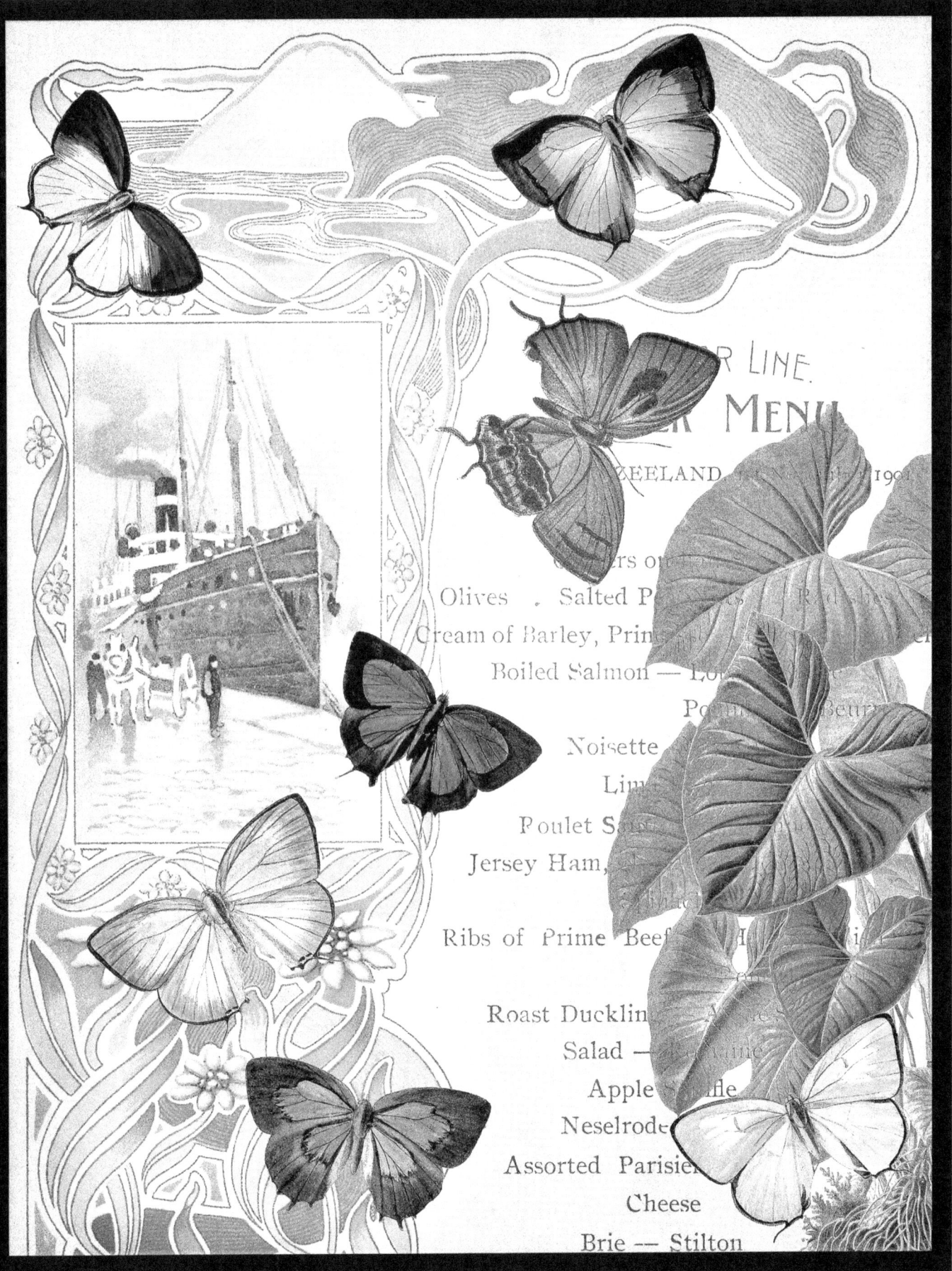

R LINE.
MENU

ZEELAND ... 1901

Olives . Salted P... R...
Cream of Barley, Prin...
Boiled Salmon — L...
Po... Beur...
Noisette
Lim...
Poulet S...
Jersey Ham,
Ribs of Prime Beef
Roast Duckling
Salad —
Apple S...fle
Neselrode
Assorted Parisie...
Cheese
Brie -- Stilton

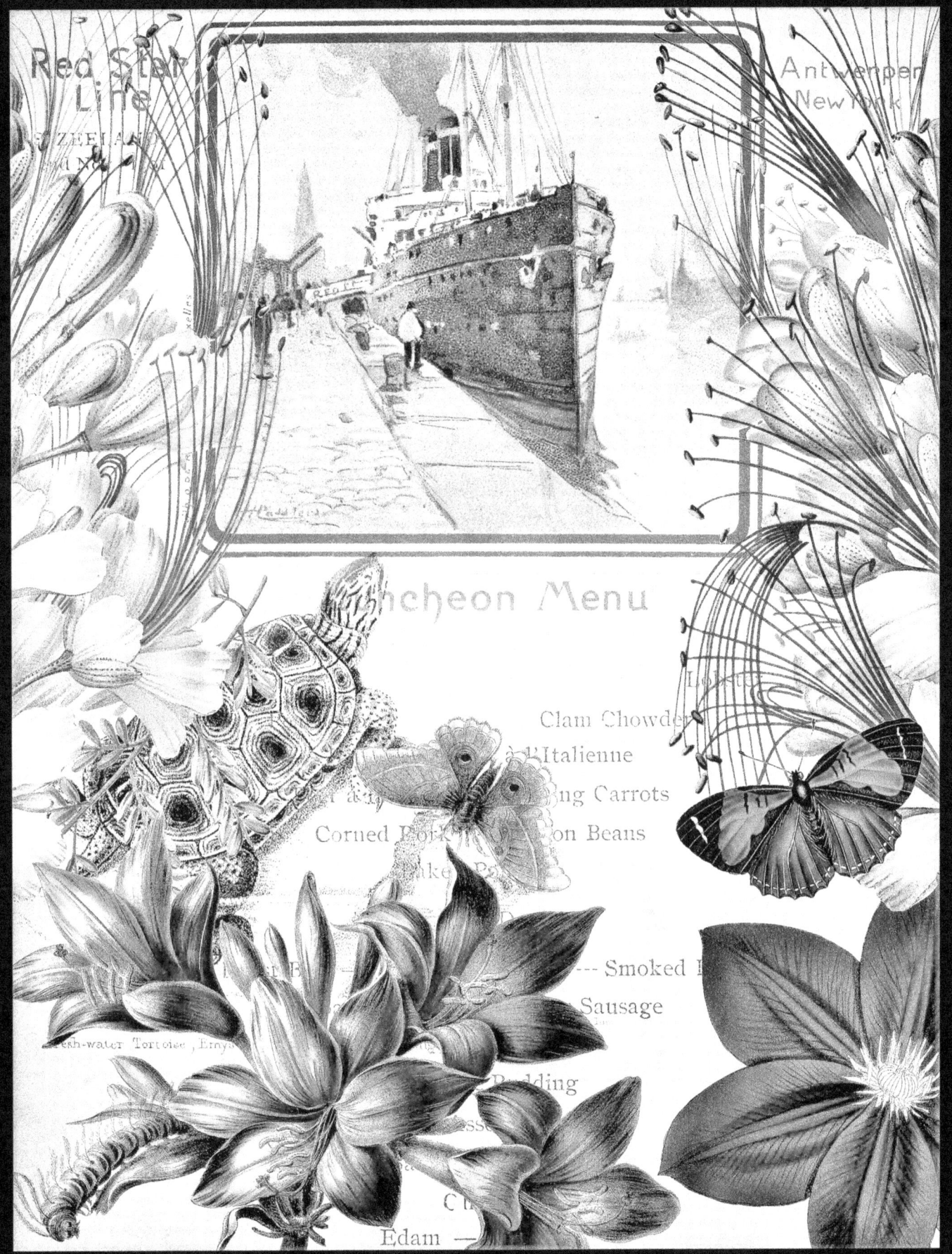

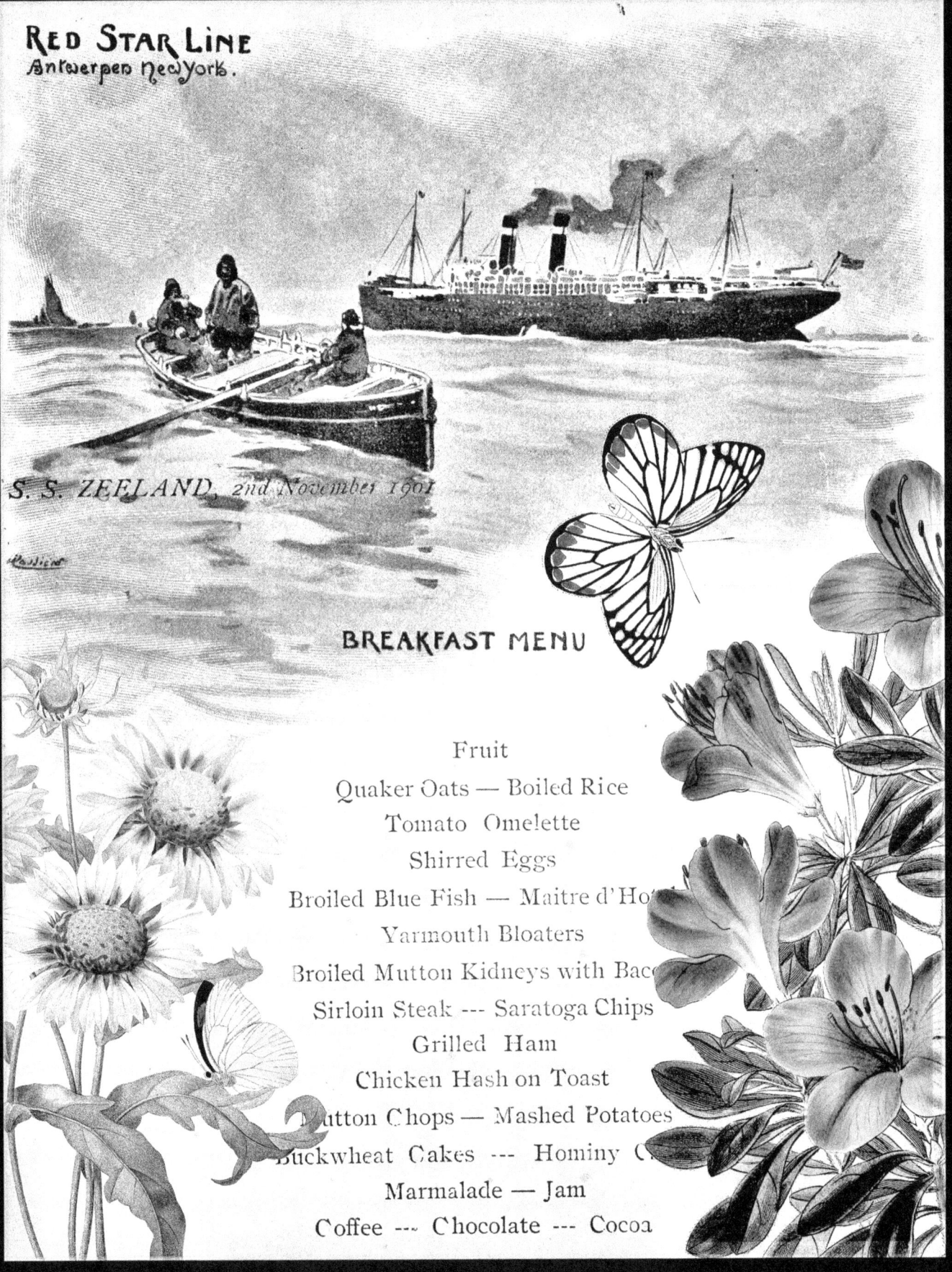

RED STAR LINE
Antwerpen New York.

S.S. ZEELAND, 2nd November 1901

BREAKFAST MENU

Fruit
Quaker Oats — Boiled Rice
Tomato Omelette
Shirred Eggs
Broiled Blue Fish — Maitre d'Hotel
Yarmouth Bloaters
Broiled Mutton Kidneys with Bacon
Sirloin Steak --- Saratoga Chips
Grilled Ham
Chicken Hash on Toast
Mutton Chops — Mashed Potatoes
Buckwheat Cakes --- Hominy
Marmalade — Jam
Coffee --- Chocolate --- Cocoa

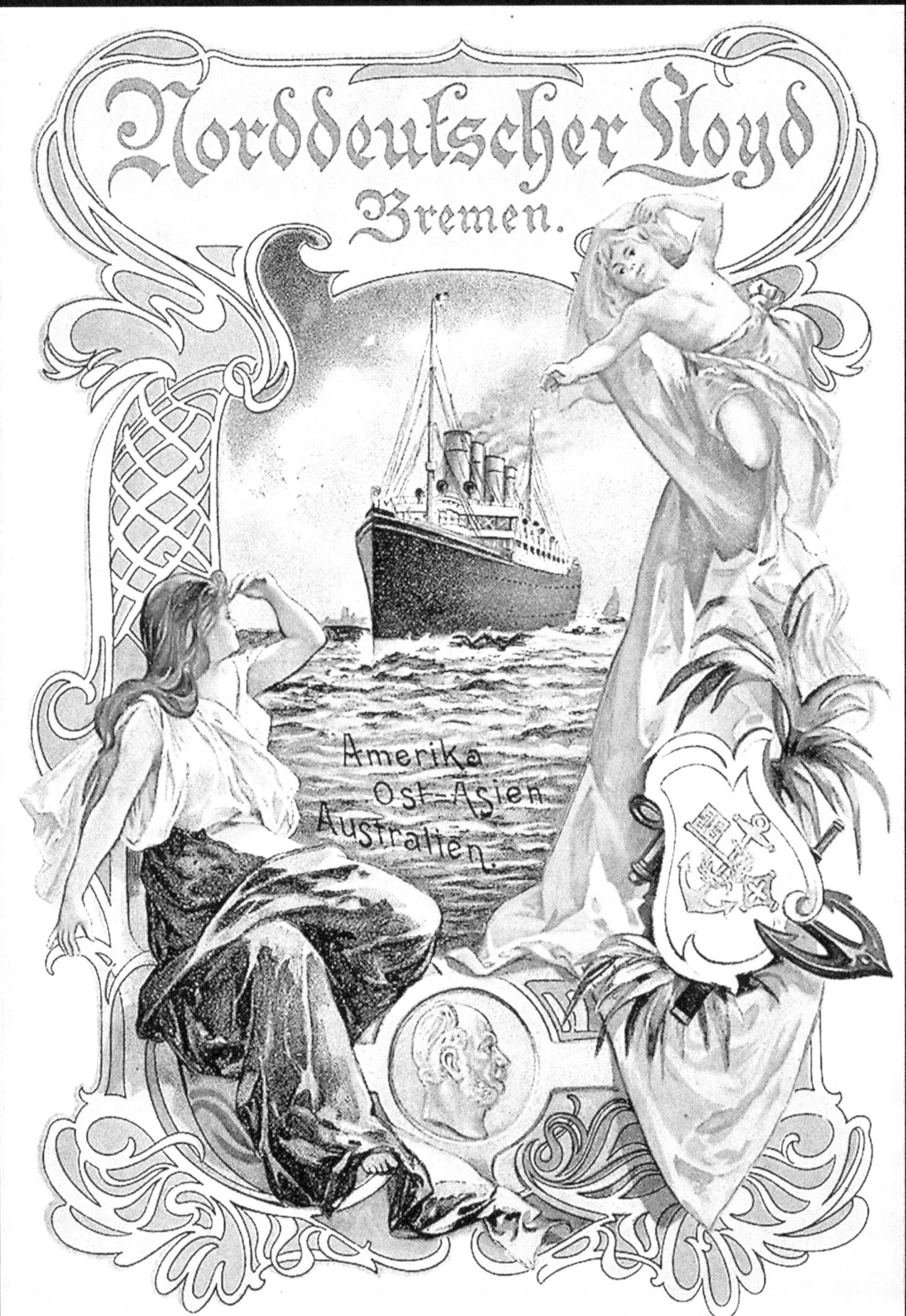

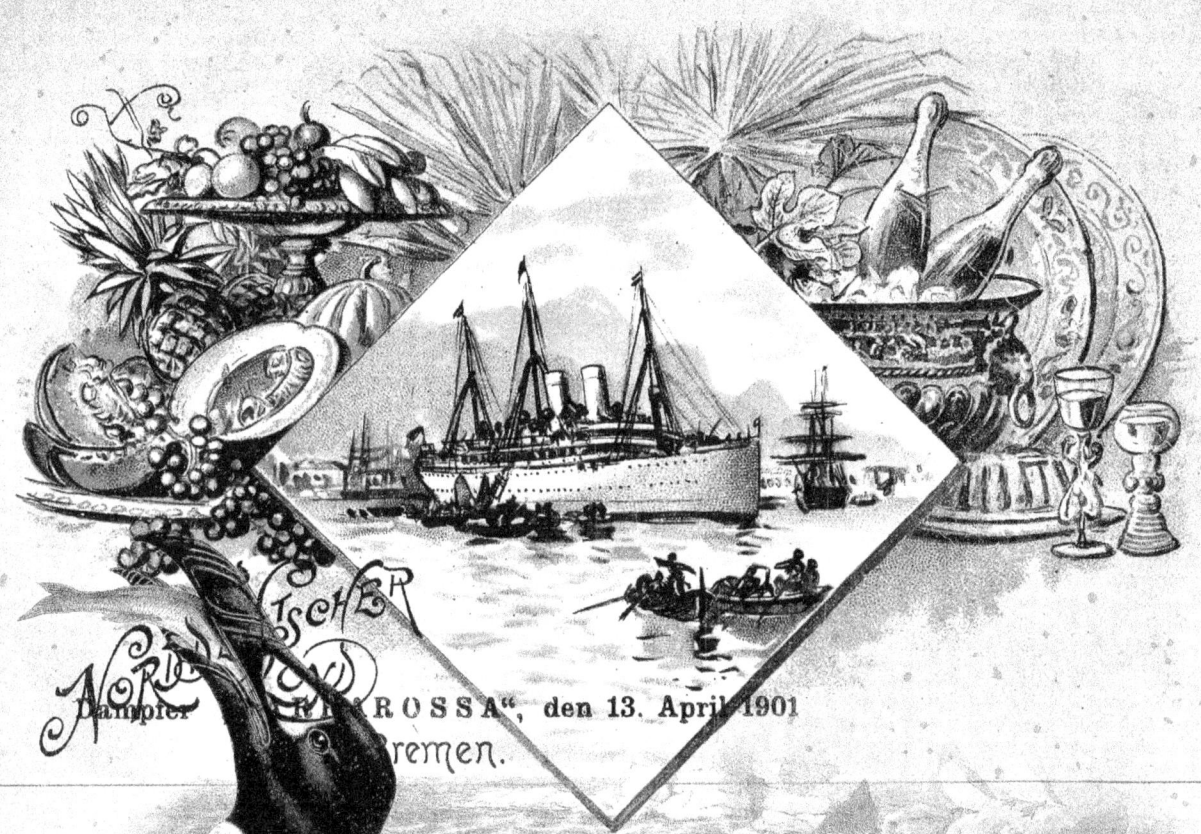

Norddeutscher Lloyd
Dampfer "Barbarossa", den 13. April 1901
Bremen.

Lunch.

Geb. Kalbsknorpeln, Rémouladensauce	Fried veal kernels, Sauce rémoulade
Pellkartoffeln, Speck-Sauce	Jacket potatoes, Bacon sauce
Thee	Tea
B...	...
Sch... Zungenwurst	Tongue sausage
Zu... gekochter ...	Boiled ham
... Heringe	Pickled herrings
Kartoffel-Herings Salat	Potato Herring salad
Rote...	Beetroots
Rahm Käse	Cream cheese

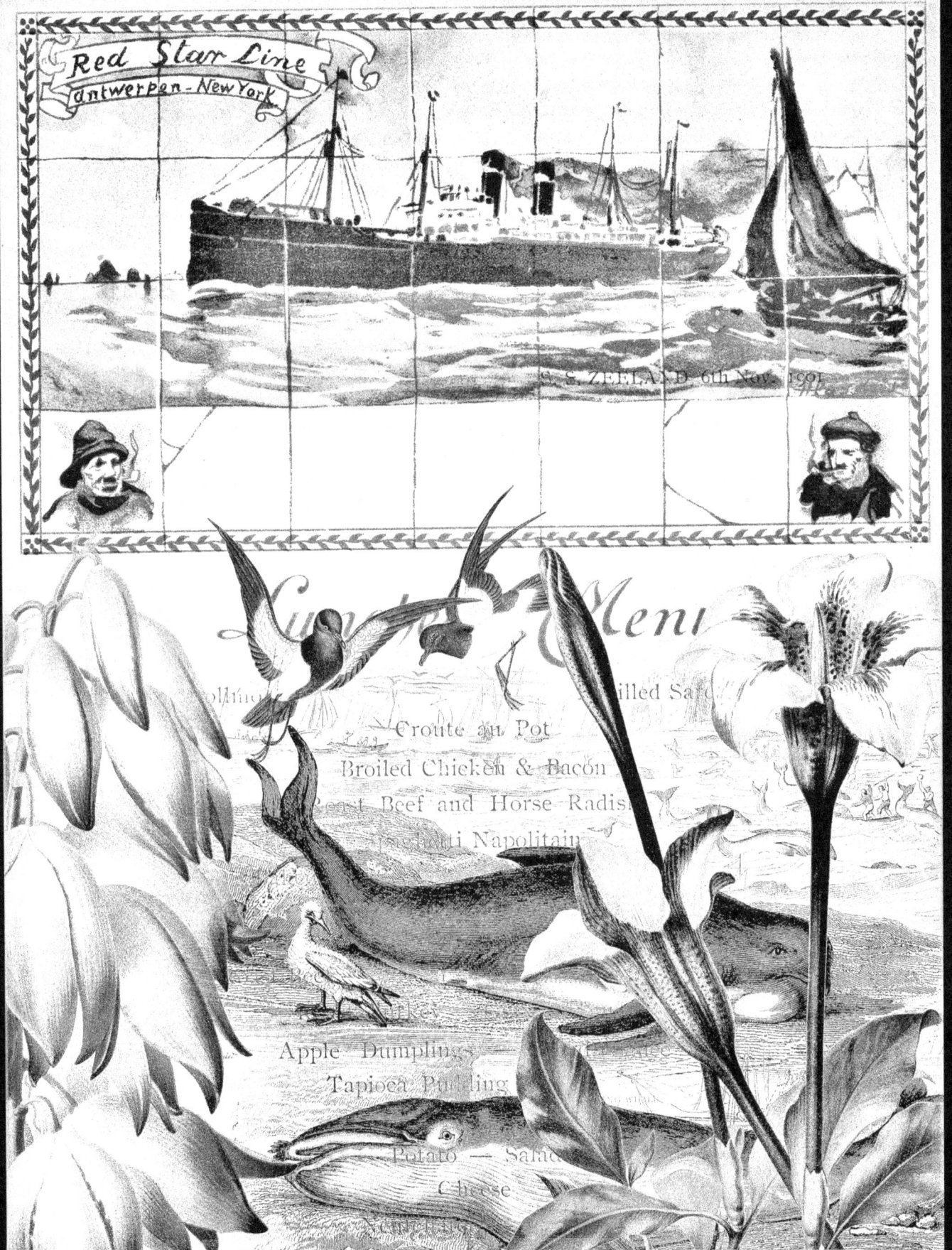

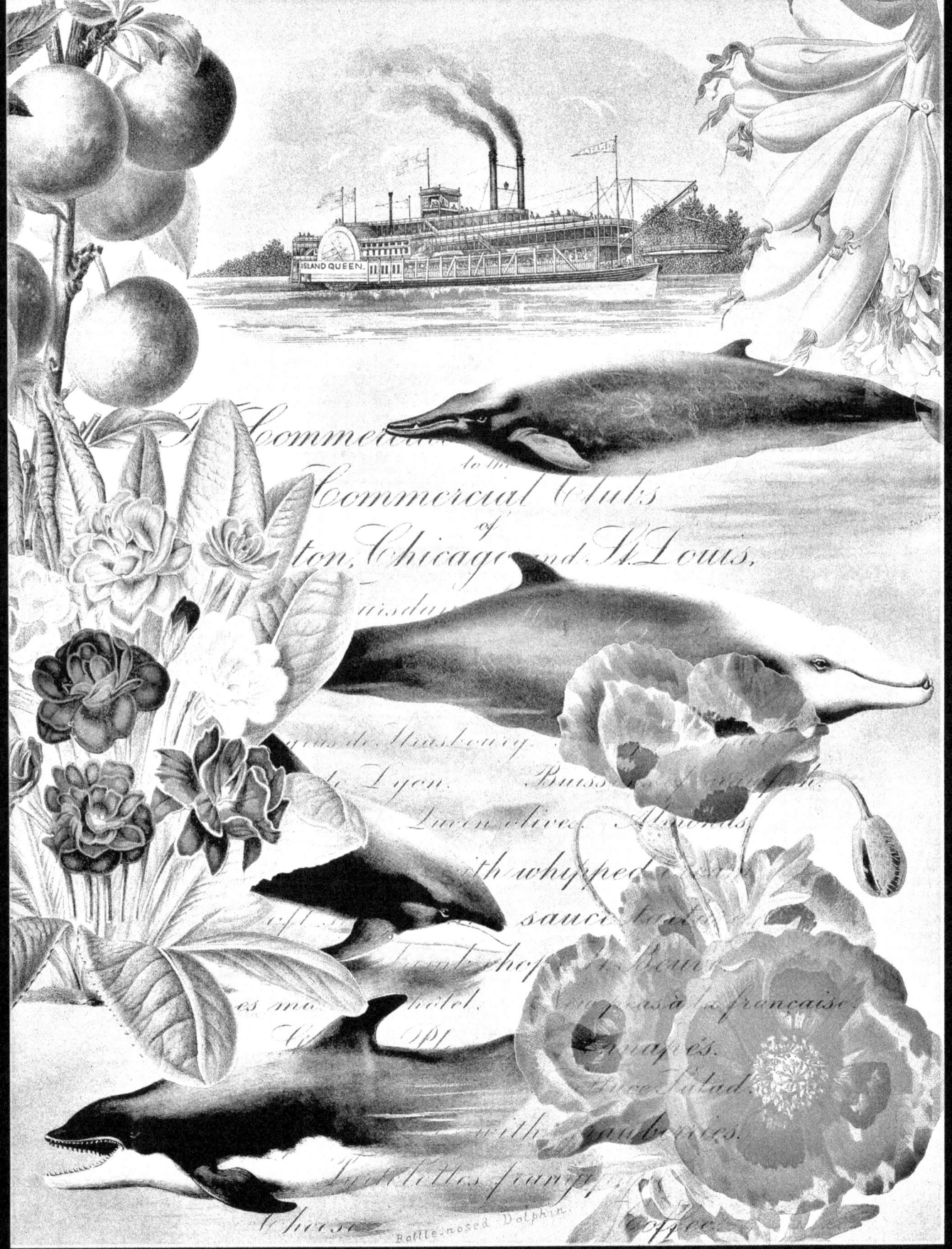

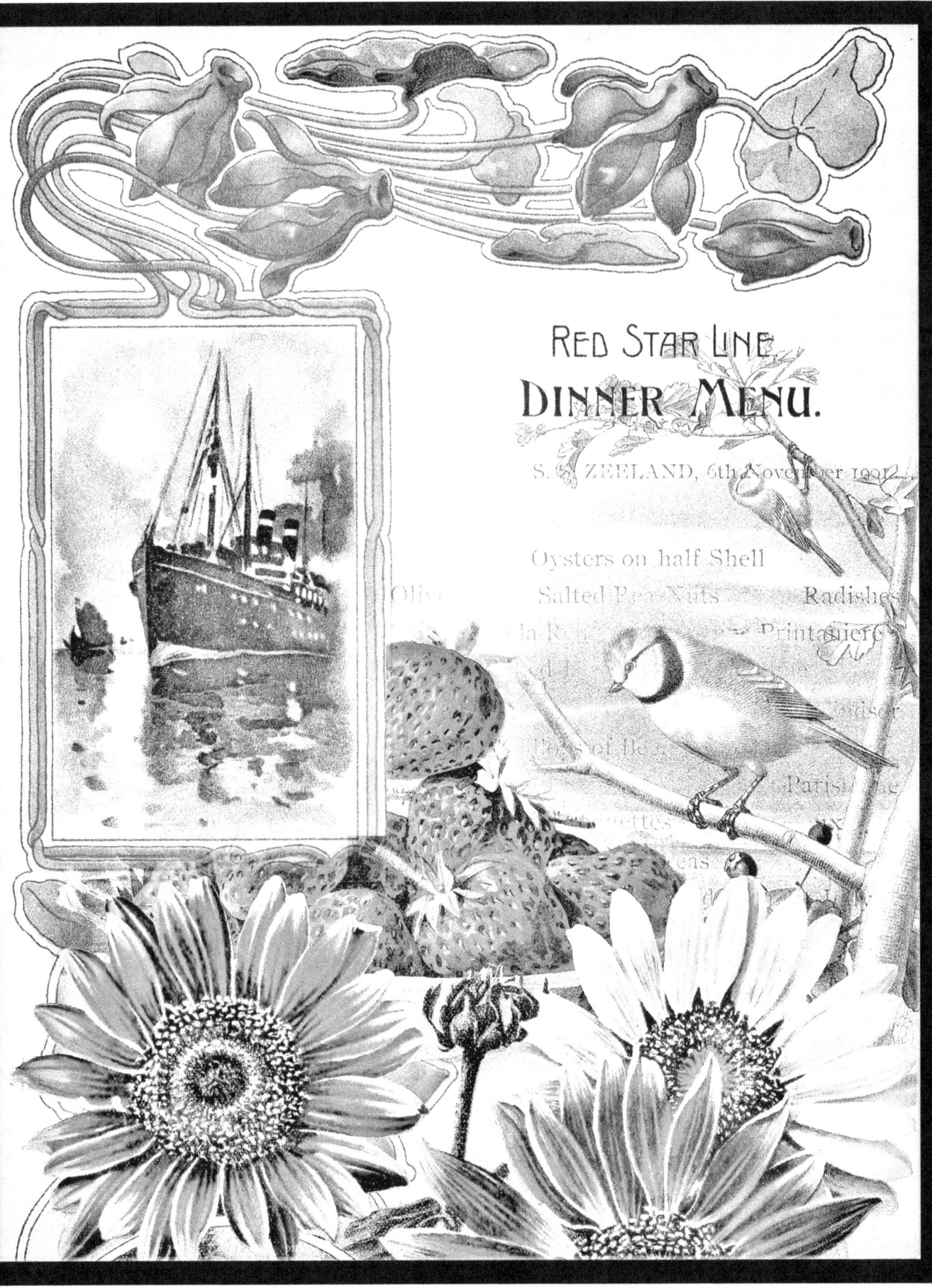

Red Star Line
Dinner Menu.

S.S. ZEELAND, 6th November 1901

Oysters on half Shell
Salted Pea Nuts   Radishes

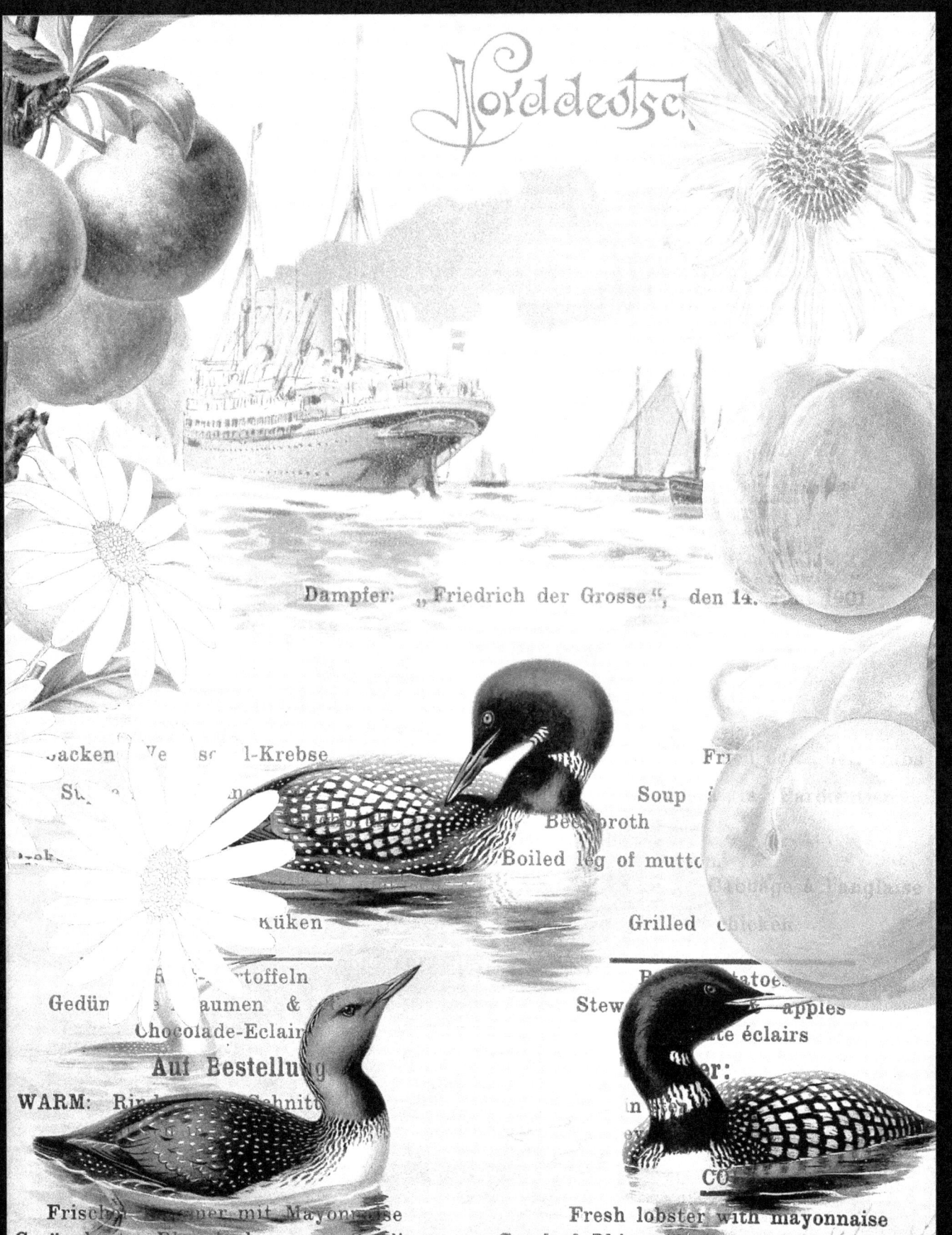

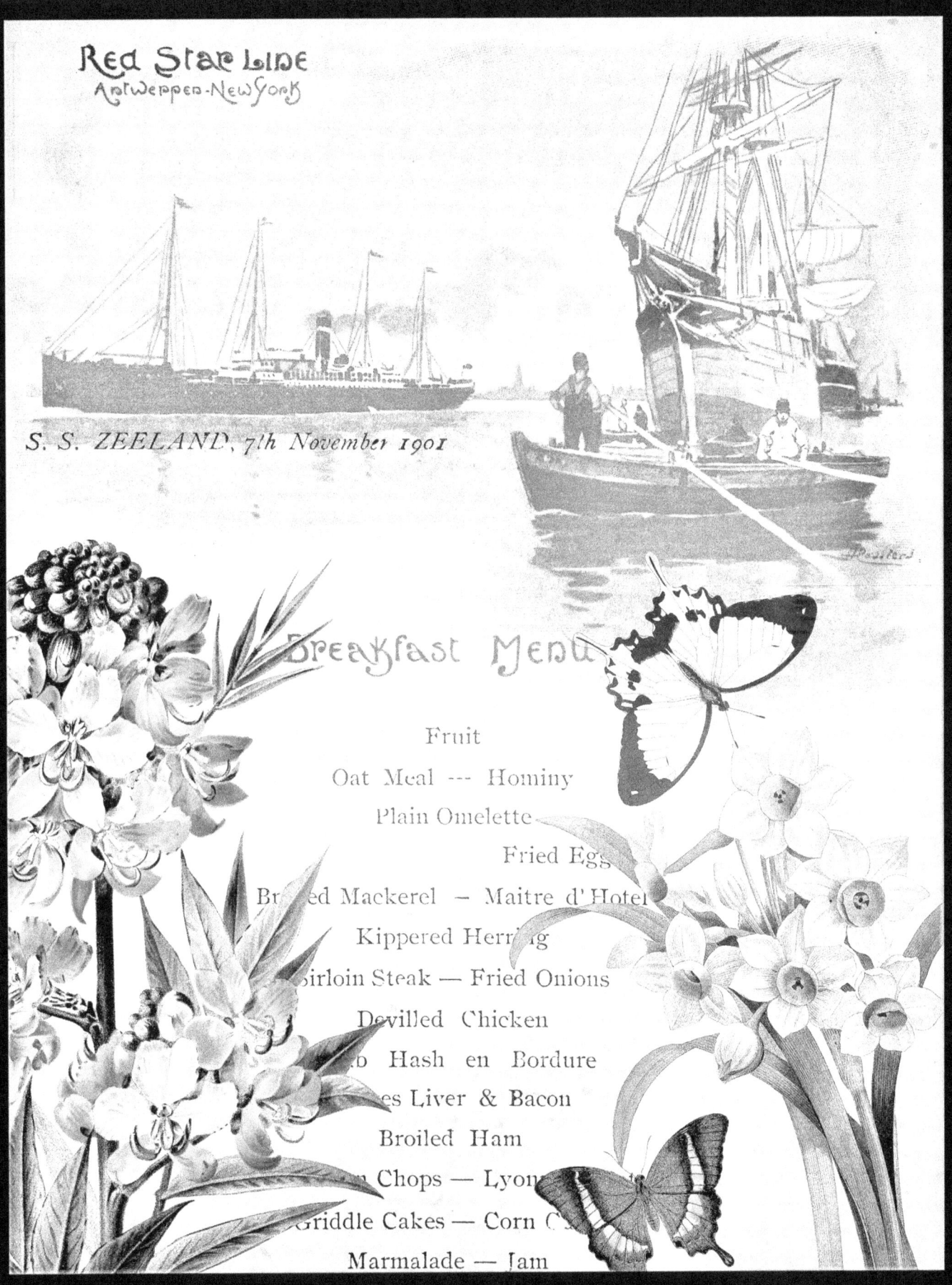

Red Star Line
Antwerpen-New York

S.S. ZEELAND, 7th November 1901

Breakfast Menu

Fruit

Oat Meal --- Hominy

Plain Omelette

Fried Eggs

Broiled Mackerel — Maitre d'Hotel

Kippered Herring

Sirloin Steak — Fried Onions

Devilled Chicken

Hash en Bordure

Liver & Bacon

Broiled Ham

Chops — Lyonnaise

Griddle Cakes — Corn Cakes

Marmalade — Jam

Norddeutscher Lloyd Bremen.

Amerika-Asien-Australien.

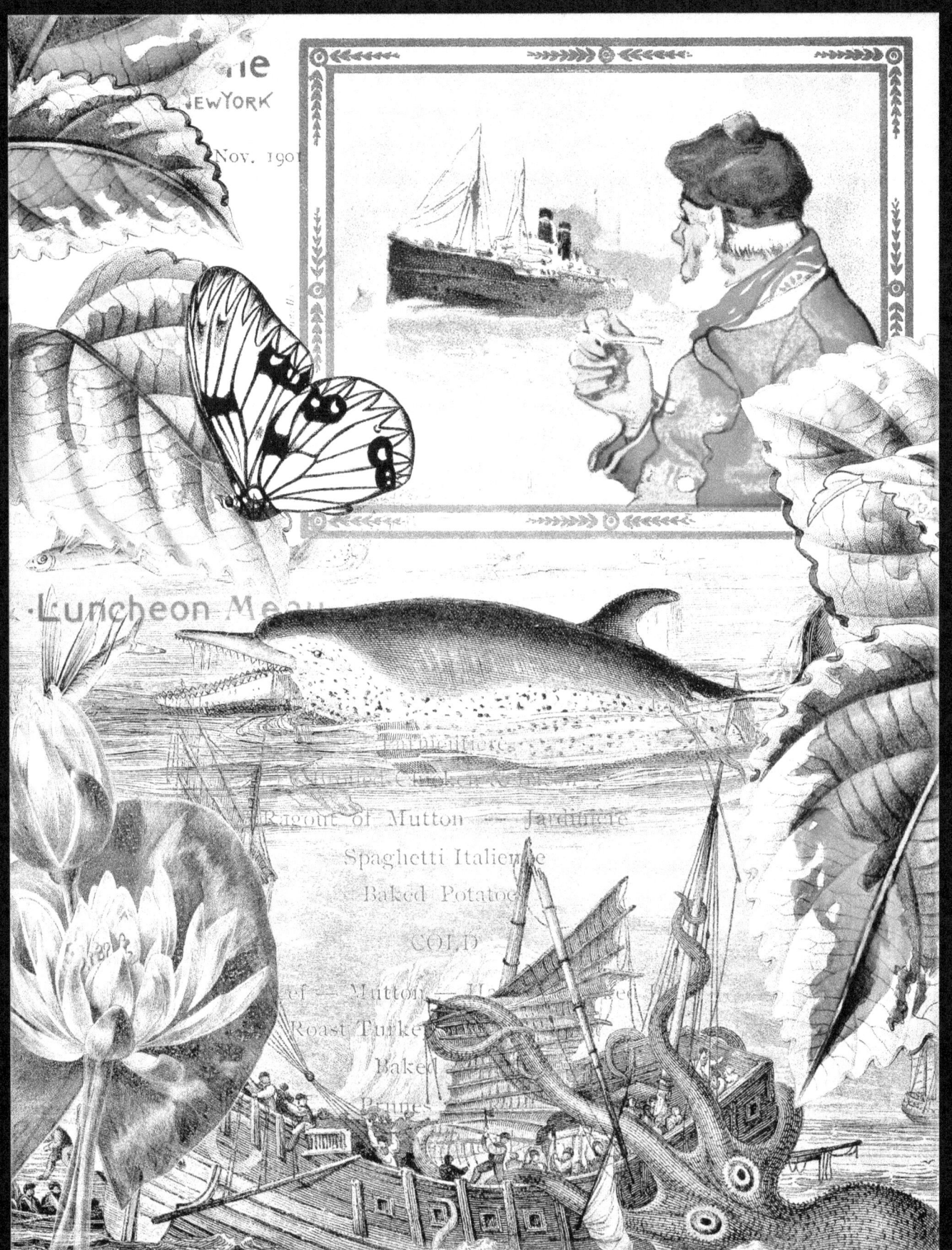

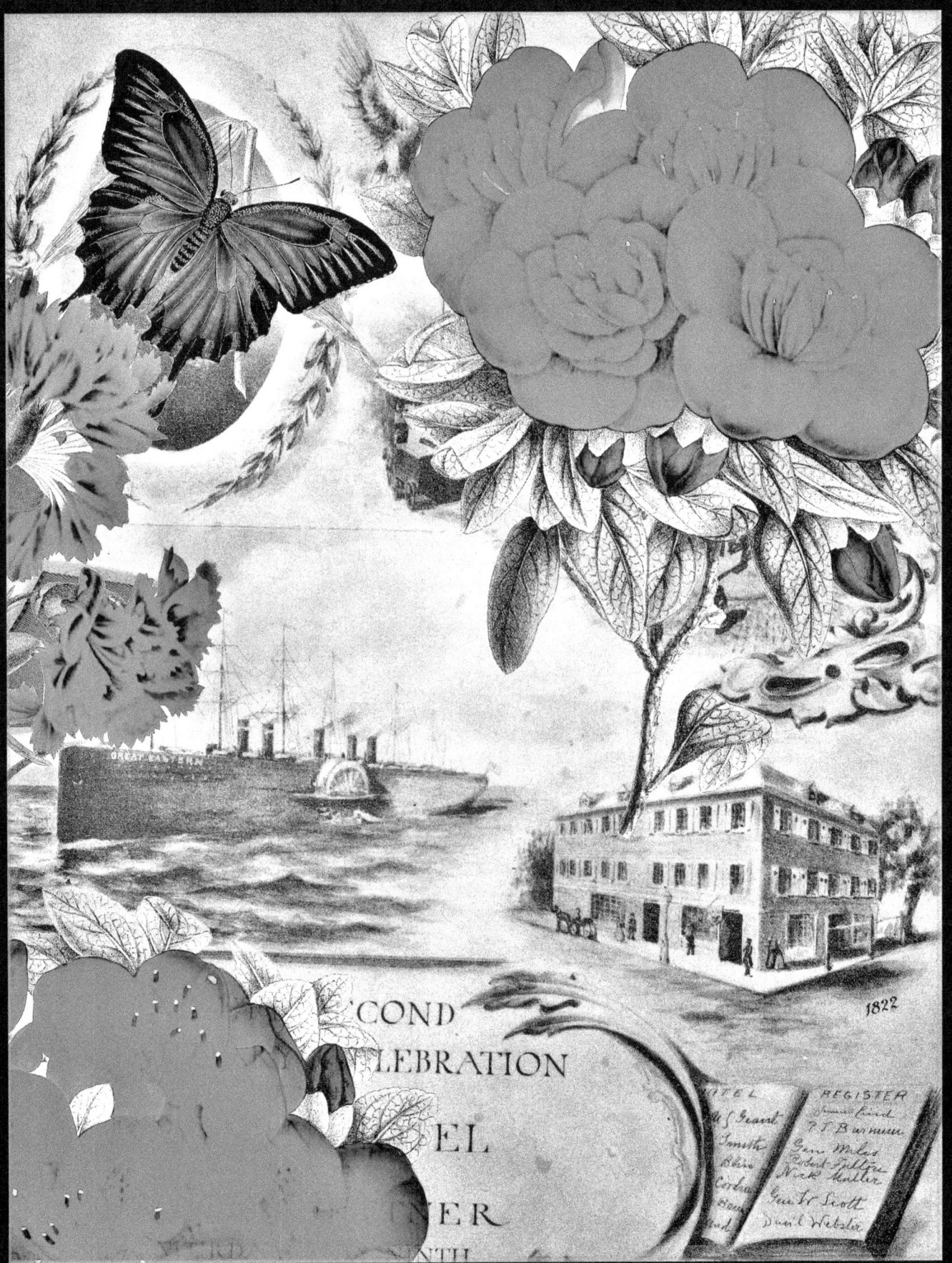

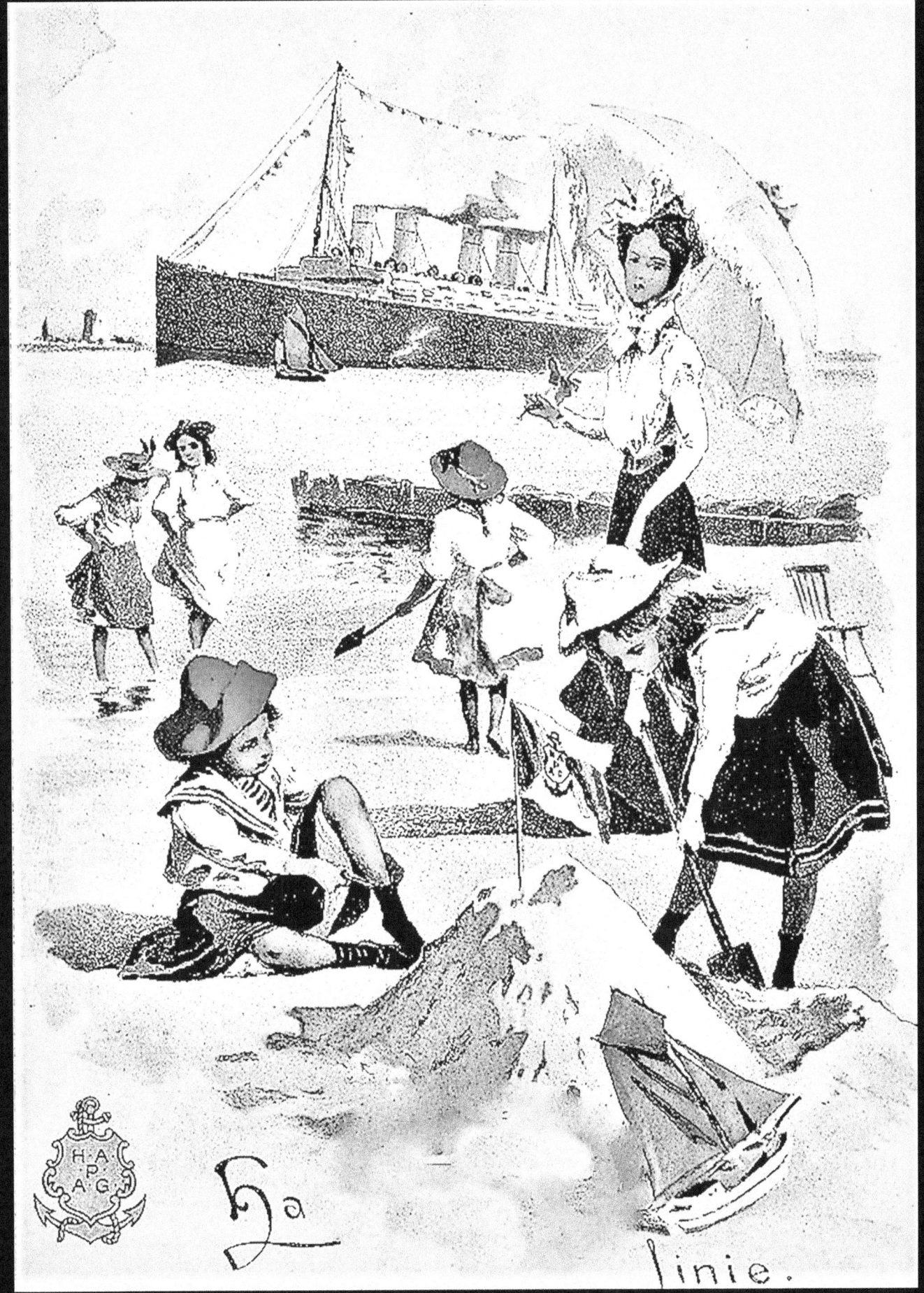

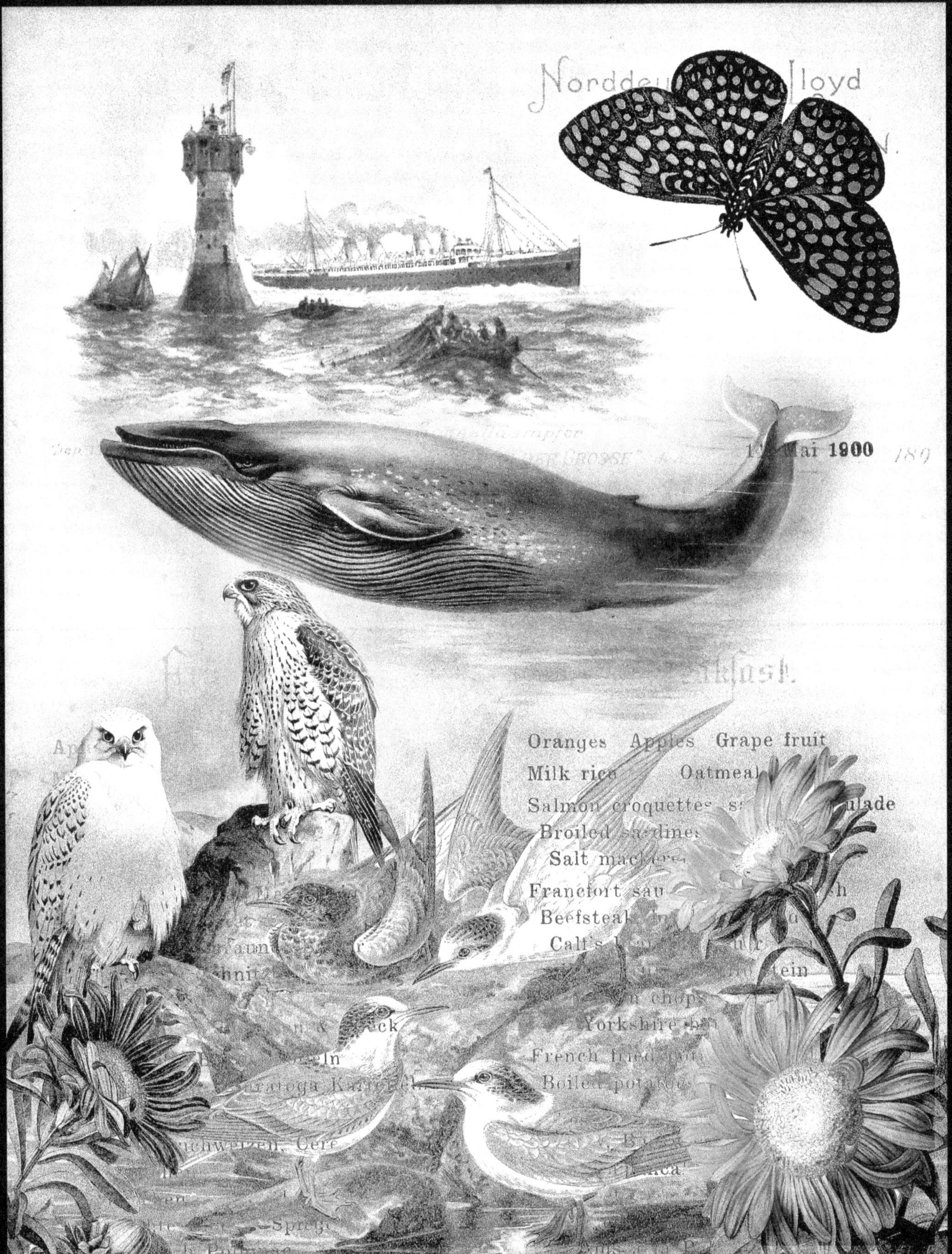

Norddeu... lloyd

...Mai **1900** 189

Breakfast.

Oranges   Apples   Grape fruit
Milk rice   Oatmeal
Salmon croquettes   ...ulade
Broiled sardines
Salt mackerel
Francfort sau...
Beefsteak
Calf's
            ...tein
            ...chops
            Yorkshire ...
French fried ...
Boiled potatoes

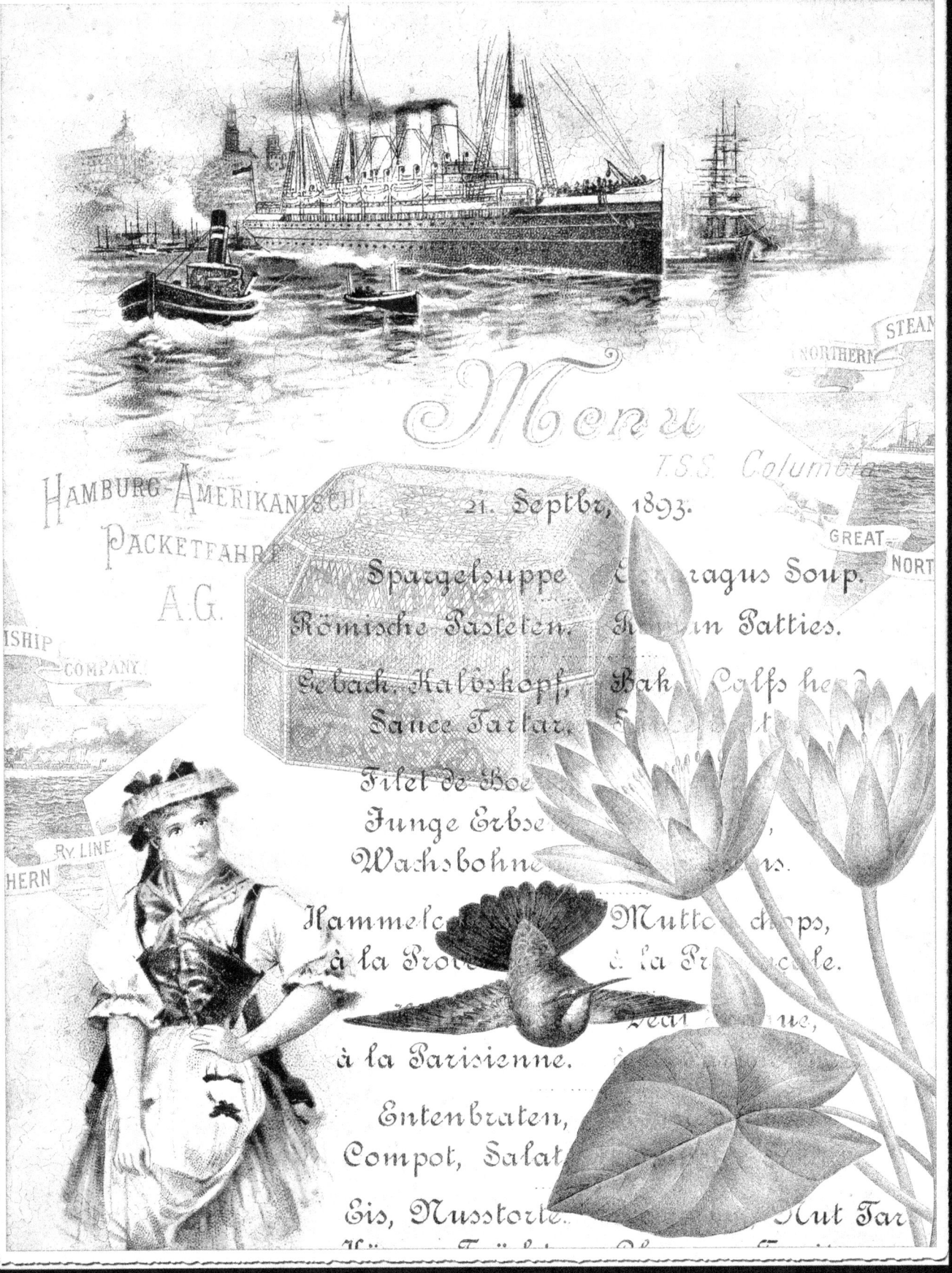

Menu

T.S.S. Columbia

Hamburg-Amerikanische Packetfahrt A.G.

21. Septbr. 1893.

Spargelsuppe — Asparagus Soup.
Römische Pasteten. — Roman Patties.
Gebach. Kalbskopf, — Bak. Calfs head
Sauce Tartar.

Filet de Bœuf
Junge Erbsen
Wachsbohnen

Hammelchops, — Mutton chops,
à la Provençale. — à la Provençale.

à la Parisienne.

Entenbraten,
Compot, Salat
Eis, Nusstorte. — Nut Tart

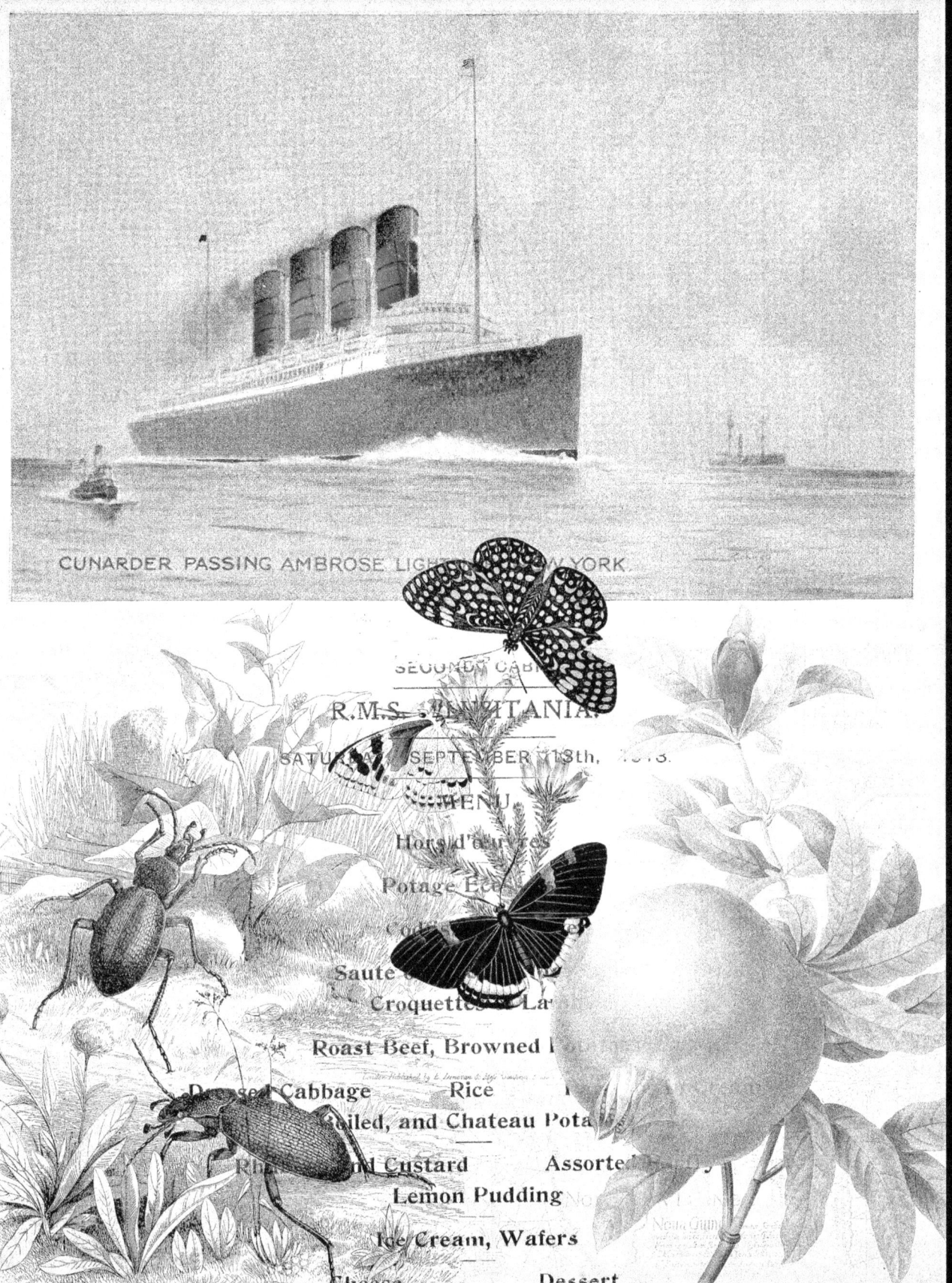

Norddeutscher Lloyd Bremen.

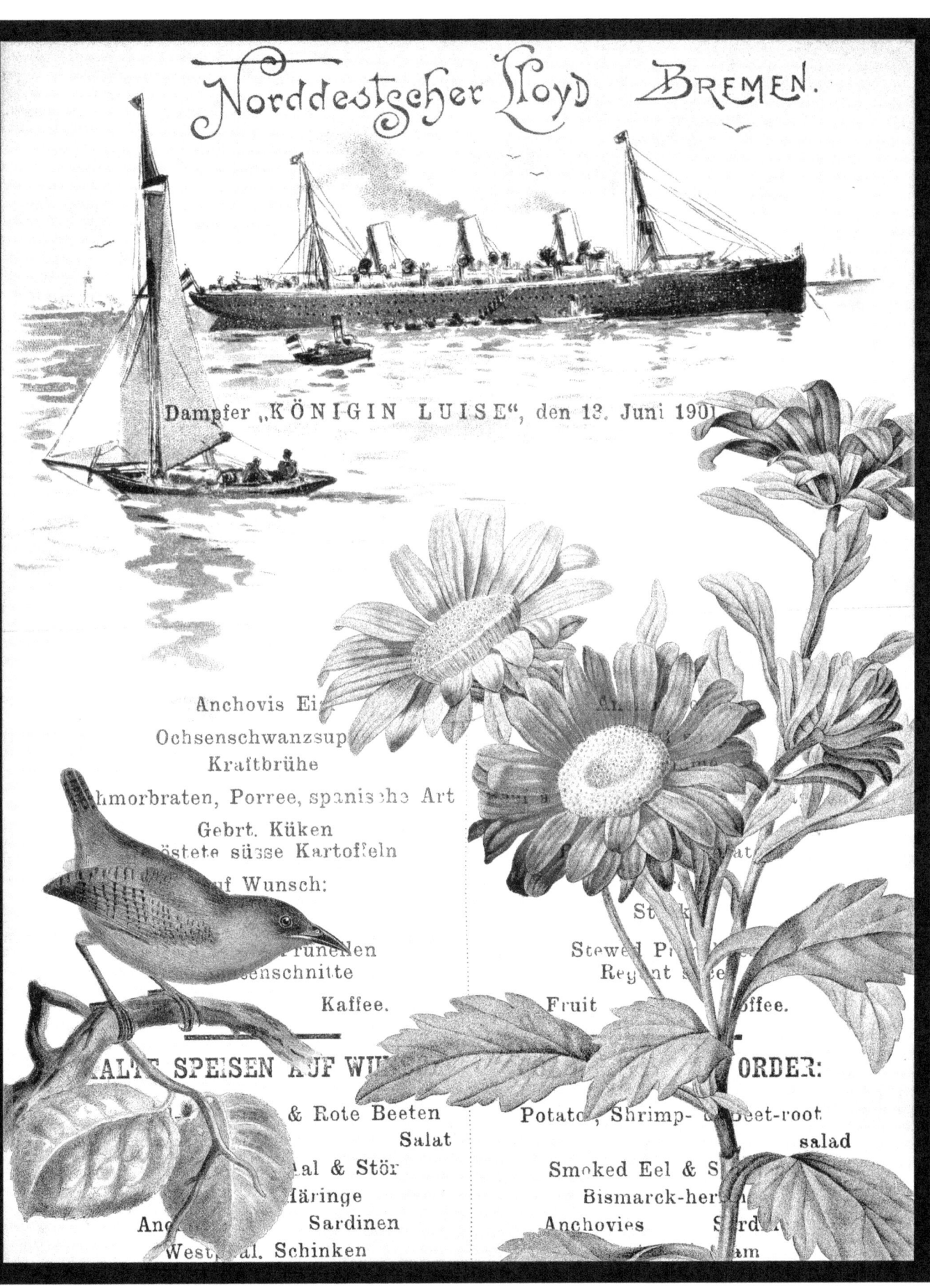

Dampfer „KÖNIGIN LUISE", den 13. Juni 1901

Anchovis Ei...
Ochsenschwanzsup...
Kraftbrühe
...hmorbraten, Porree, spanische Art
Gebrt. Küken
...östete süsse Kartoffeln
...uf Wunsch:

...runellen
...senschnitte
Kaffee.

Stewed P...
Reg...nt...
Fruit ...ffee.

...ALTE SPEISEN AUF WU... ...ORDER:

& Rote Beeten   Potato, Shrimp- ...beet-root
        Salat   salad
...al & Stör   Smoked Eel & S...
    Häringe   Bismarck-her...
Anc...   Sardinen   Anchovies   S...d...
West...al. Schinken   ...am

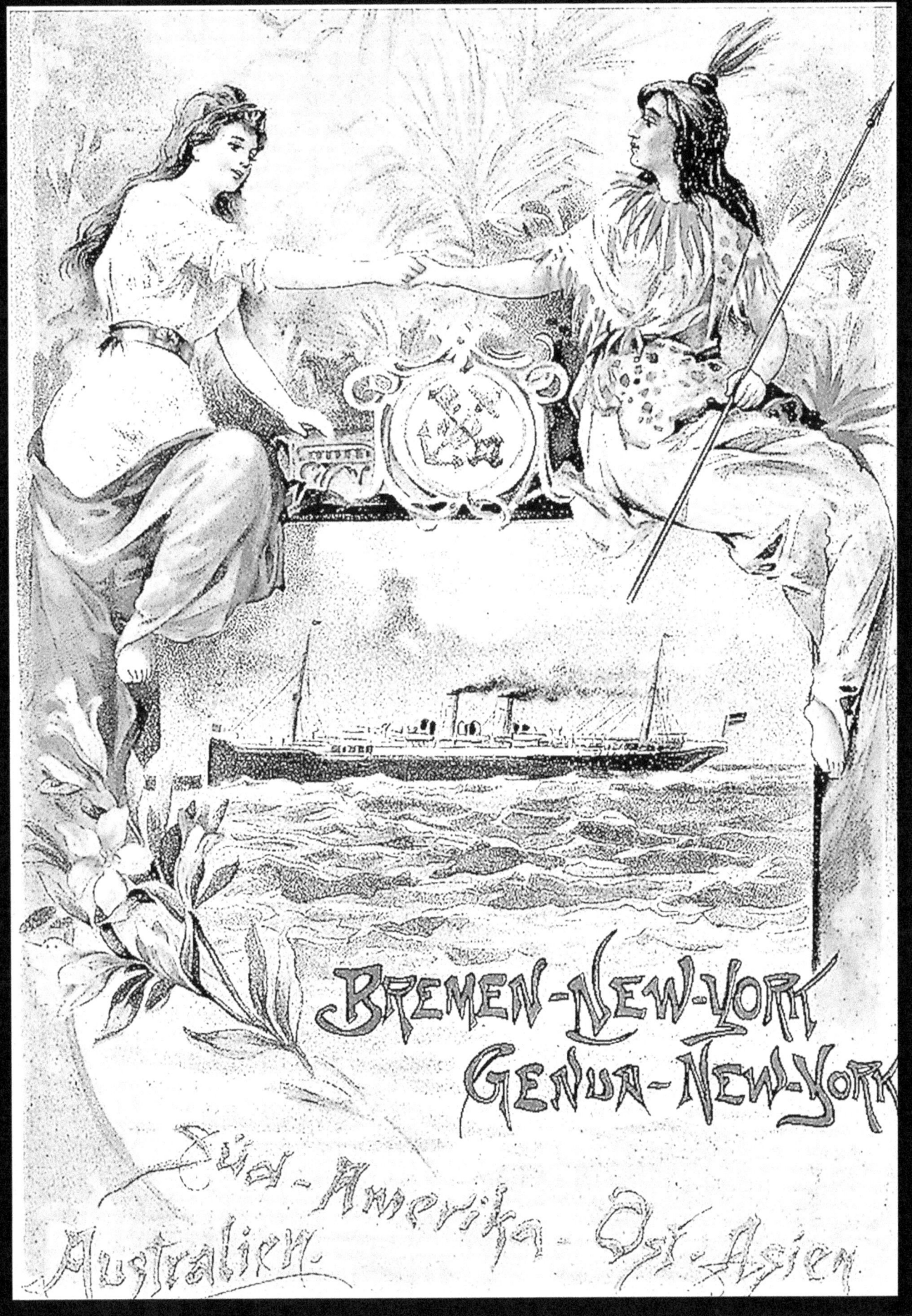

Norddeutscher Lloyd Bremen.

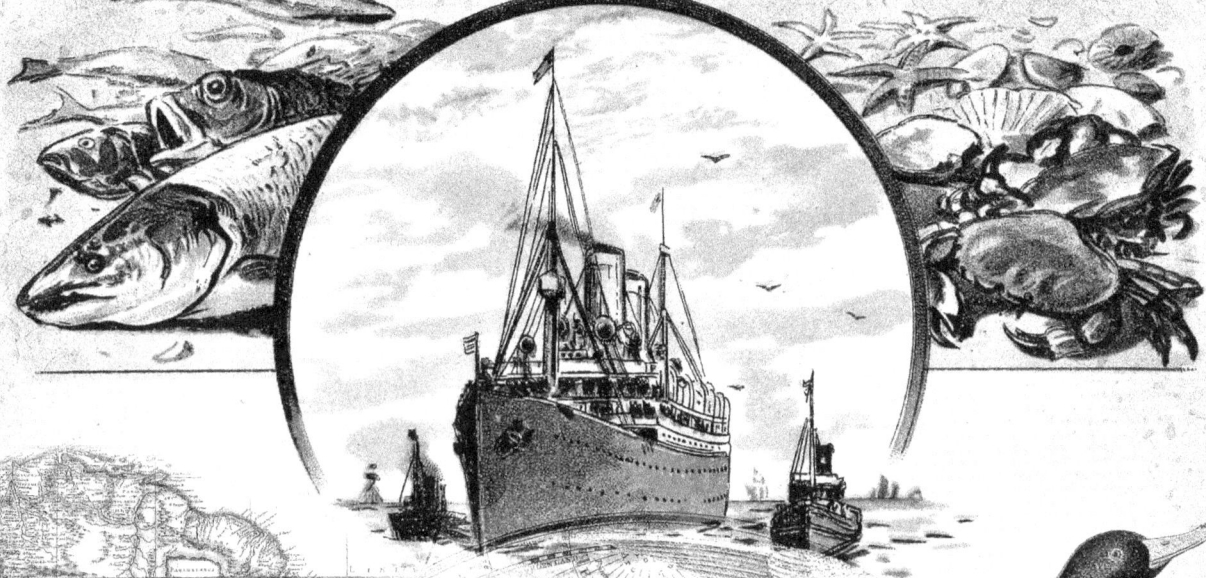

Dampfer „Kaiser Wilhelm der Grosse" .. November 1899

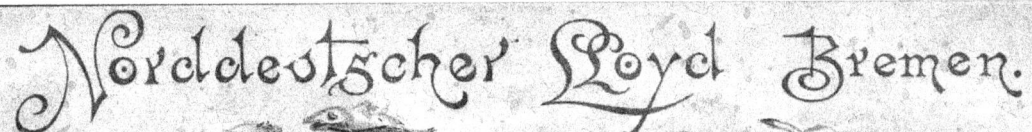

Aepfel Apfelsinen	Oranges
Grape fruit	Grape fruit
Milchreis Hafergrütze	Milkrice Oatmeal
Geback. Seezunge, Remoladen Sauce	Fried sole, sauce rémoulade
Salzmakrele	Salt mackerel
Geräucherte Häringe	Smoked herring
Schweinskotelette, Pikante Sauce	Pork chops, sauce piquante
Hammelkoteletten	
Kükenhash mit Ei	Chicken hash with egg
Nieren sautées in Madeira	Kidneys sauté au madeira
Beefsteak, geröstet	Beefsteak, broiled and fried
Yorkshire Schinken	Yorkshire ham & bacon
Französische Bratkartoffeln	Fried potatoes
Saratoga chips	Saratoga chips Boiled potatoes
Rühreier	Scrambled eggs Poached eggs
Pfannkuchen, Eier à la Polignac	German pancake. Eggs à la Polignac
Eierkuchen mit Kräutern	Omelet with fine herbs
Maisgries- & Buchweizen-Kuchen	Hominy- & buckwheat cakes
Kalt: Nagelholz Cornedbeef	Cold: Smoked beef Cornedbeef
Marmelade Gelée	Marmalade Jelly

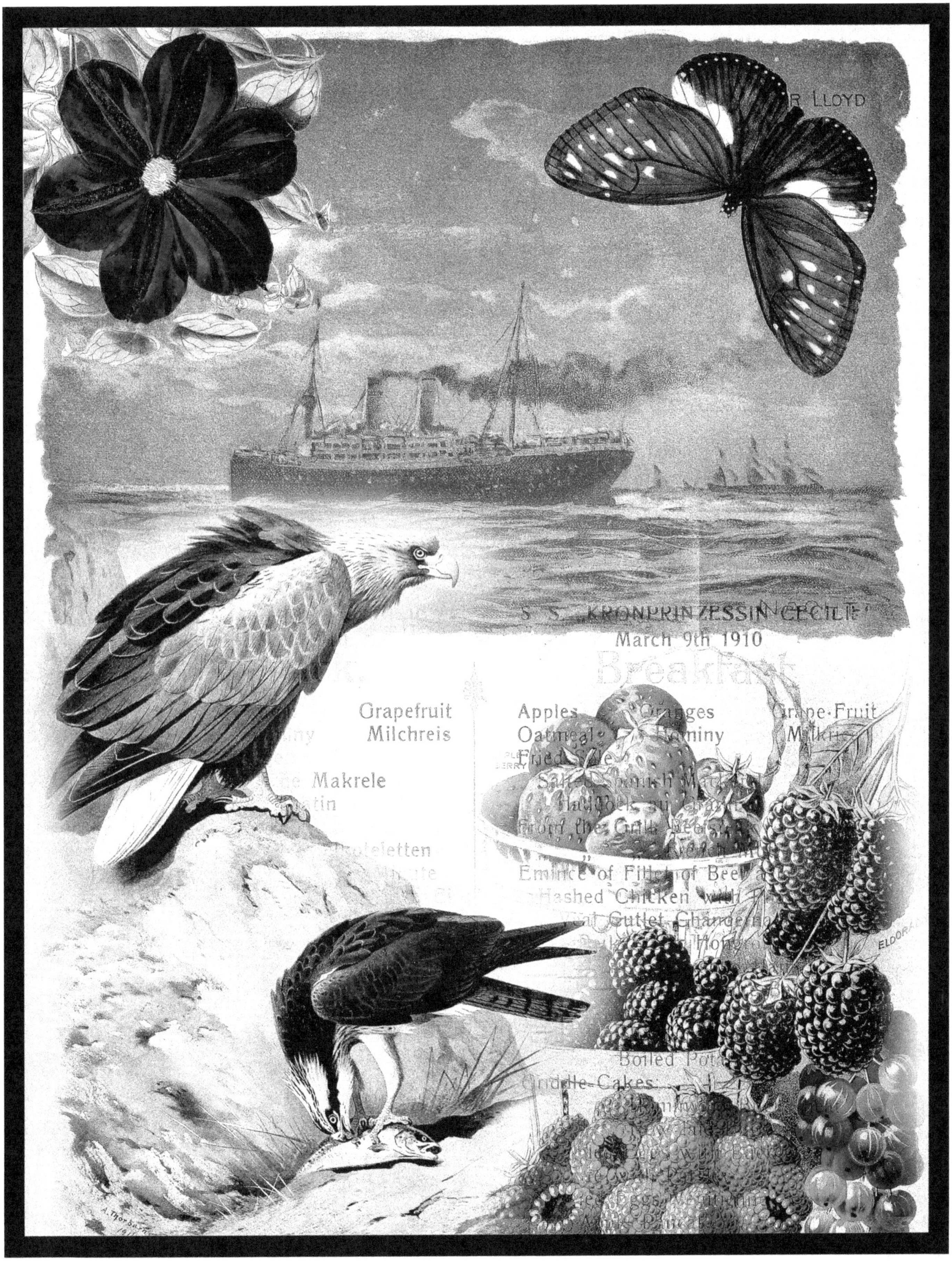

S. S. "KRONPRINZESSIN CECILIE"
March 9th 1910

Breakfast

Grapefruit   Apples   Oranges   Grape-Fruit
Milchreis   Oatmeal   Hominy   Milk

Fried Sole

Makrele   Salt Spanish M...
    Haddock...
    from the Grill...

...eletten
    Emince of Fillet of Beef
    Hashed Chicken with
    ...al Cutlet Change...

Boiled Pot...
Griddle-Cakes

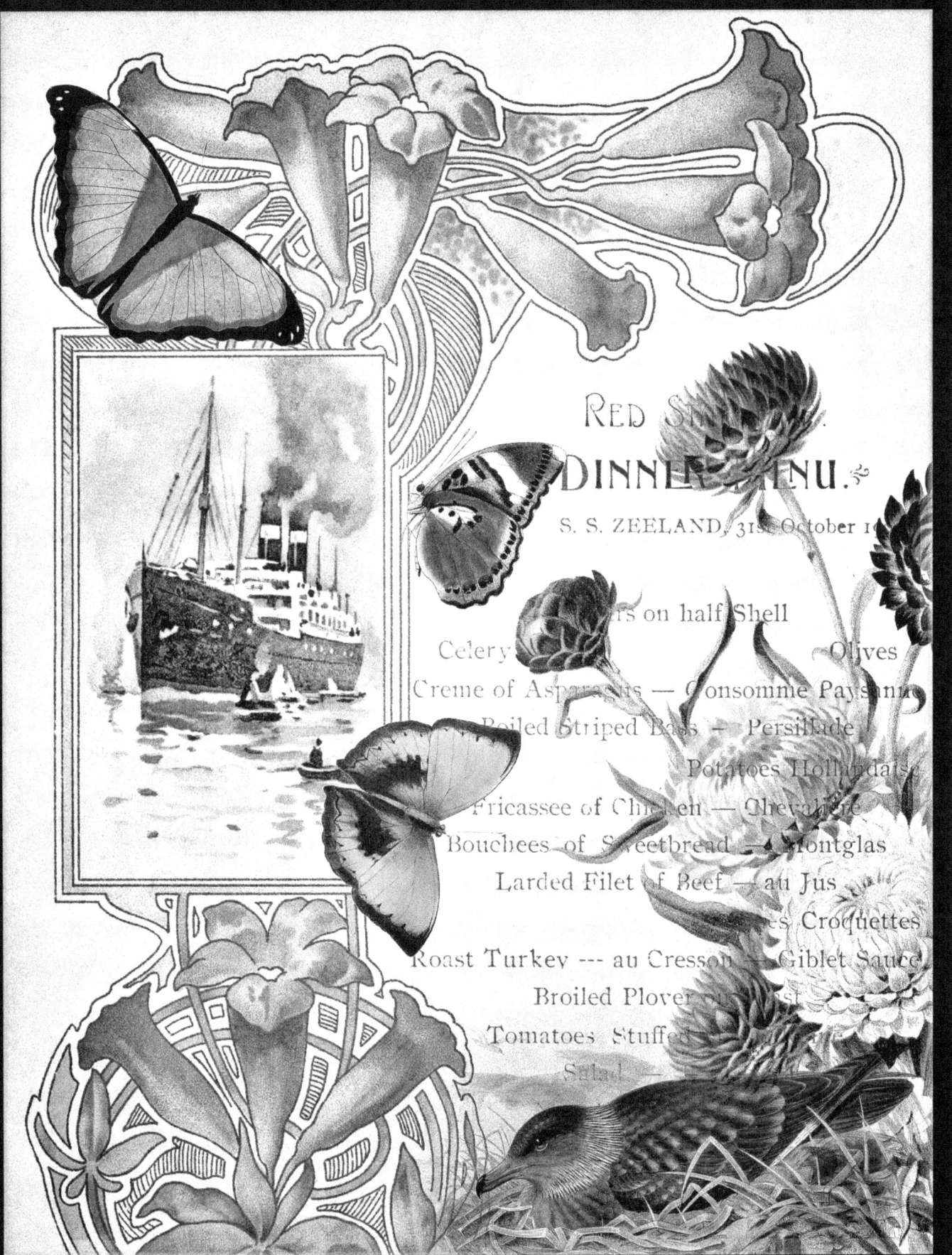

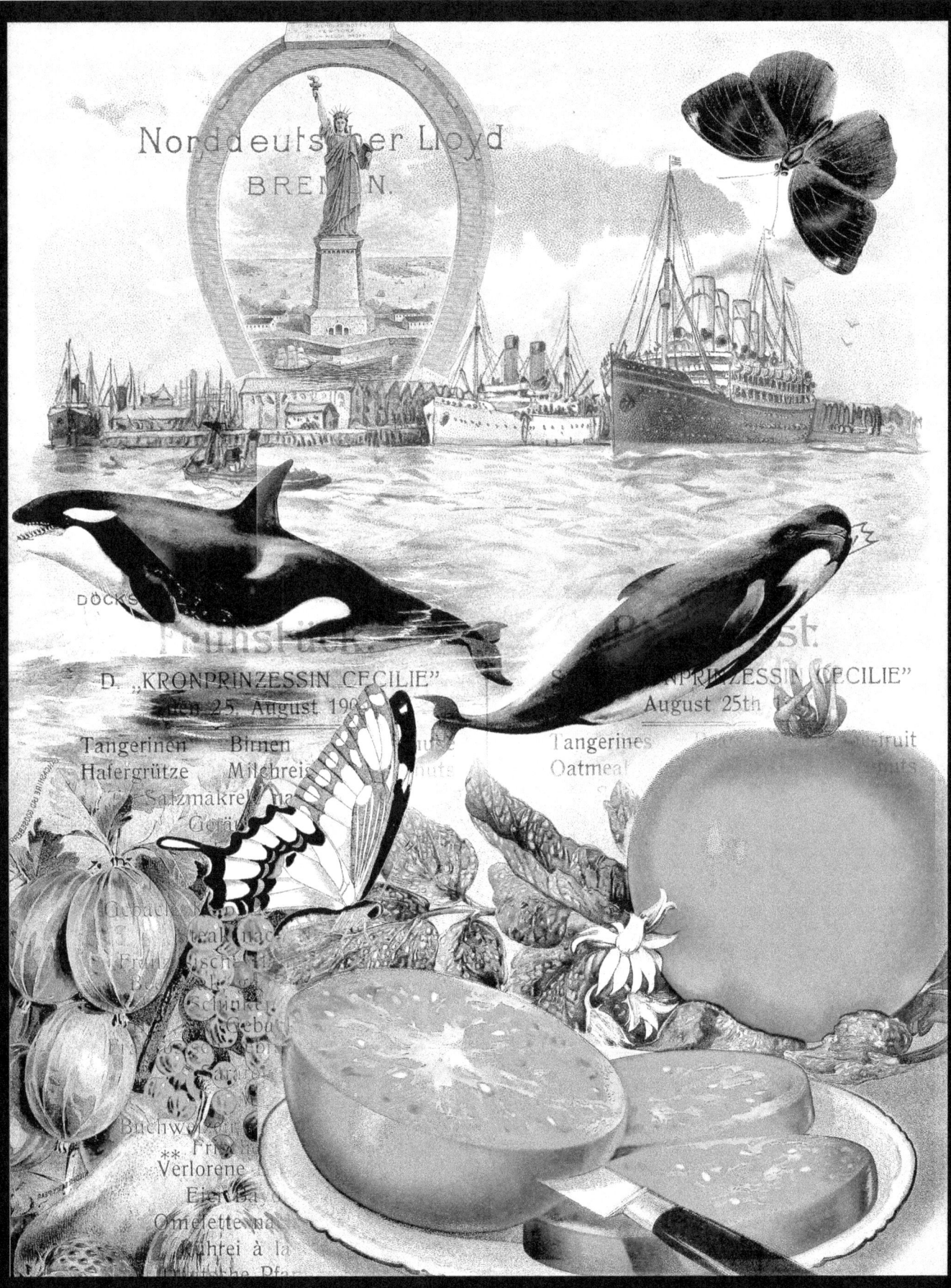

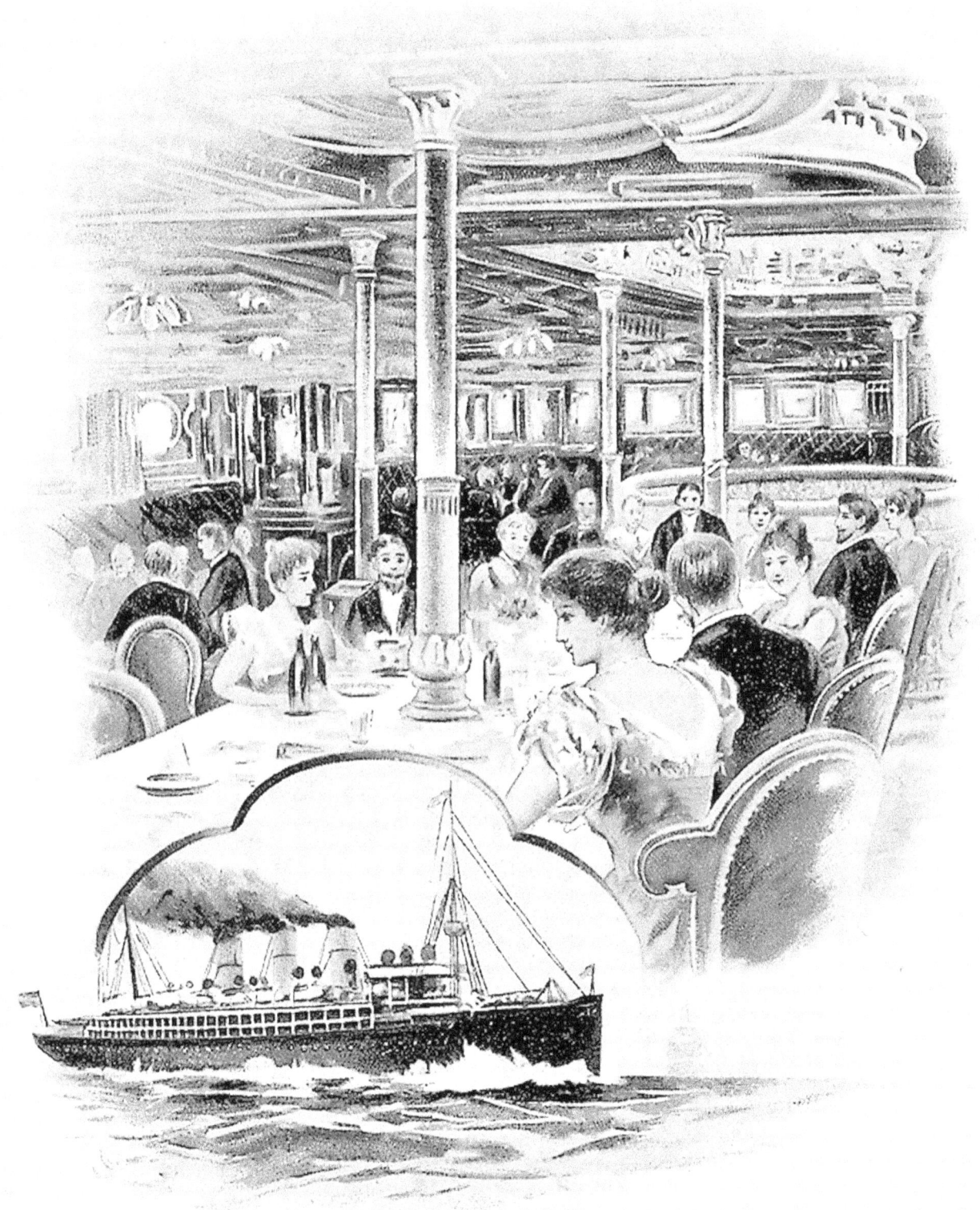

Hamburg-Amerika

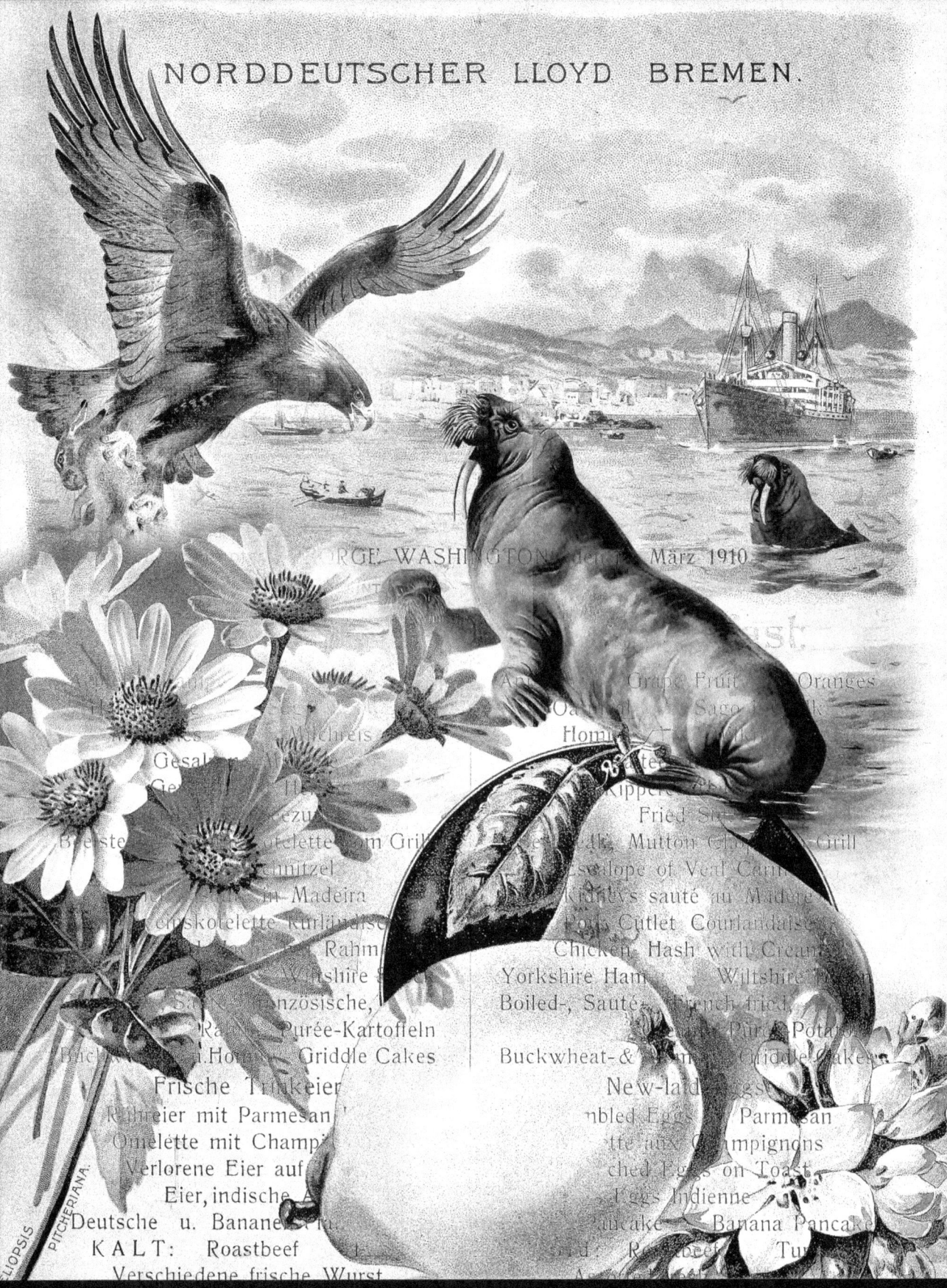

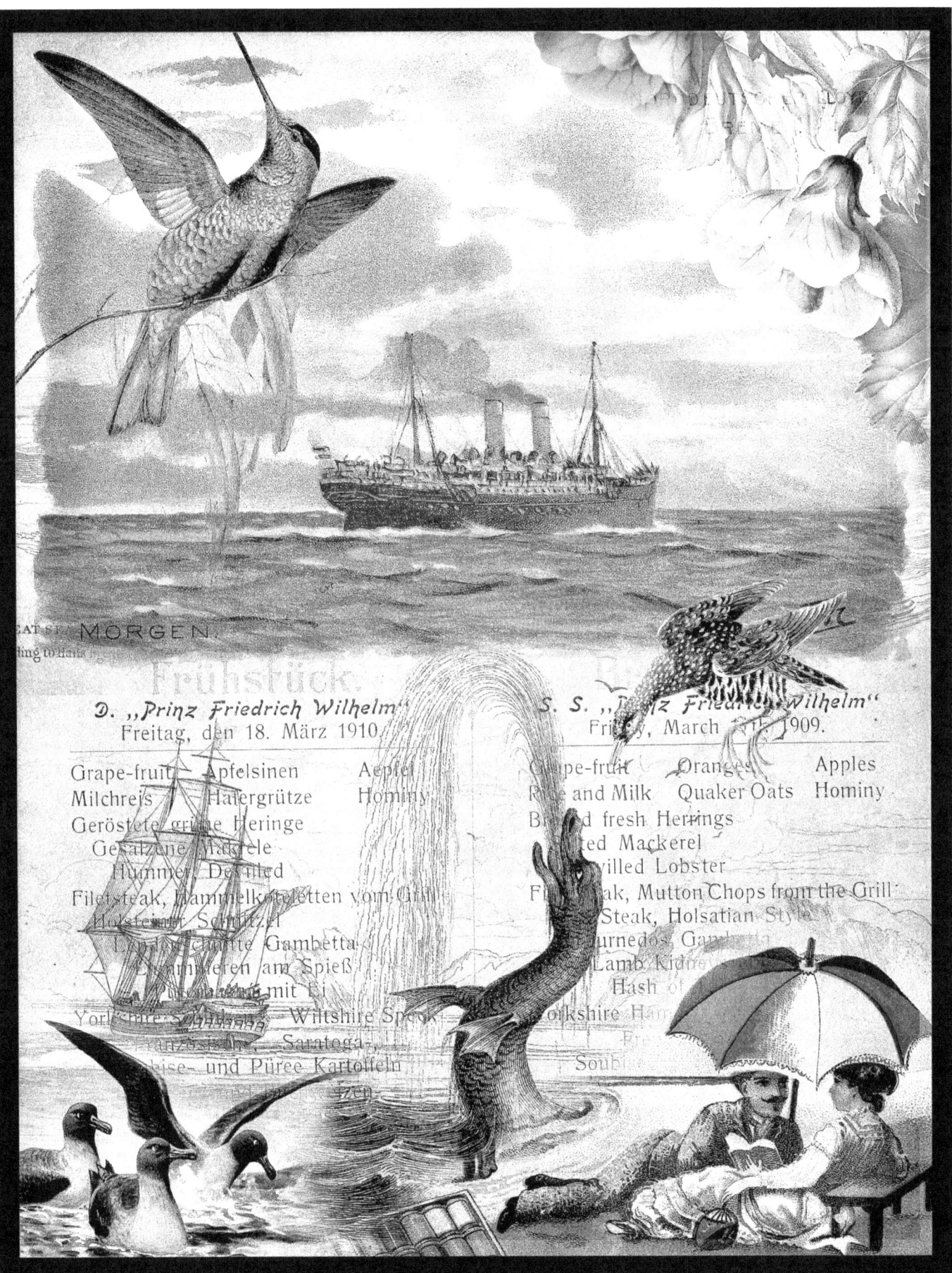

MORGEN.

Frühstück.

D. "Prinz Friedrich Wilhelm"
Freitag, den 18. März 1910.

Grape-fruit   Apfelsinen   Aepfel
Milchreis   Hafergrütze   Hominy
Geröstete grüne Heringe
Gesalzene Makrele
Hummer, Gegrillt
Filetsteak, Hammelkoteletten vom Grill
Holsteiner Schnitzel
Tournedos mit Gambetta
Lammnieren am Spieß
.... mit Ei
Yorkshire .... Wiltshire Speck
.... Saratoga
..... und Püree Kartoffeln
.........zen

S. S. "Prinz Friedrich Wilhelm"
Friday, March 18th, 1909.

Grape-fruit   Oranges   Apples
Rice and Milk   Quaker Oats   Hominy
Broiled fresh Herrings
Salted Mackerel
Grilled Lobster
Filet Steak, Mutton Chops from the Grill
..... Steak, Holsatian Style
Tournedos, Gambetta
Lamb Kidneys
Hash of
Yorkshire Ham
.....
Soubise

Dinner
in honor of the members of the
Supreme Council
Ancient Accepted Scottish Rite
and accompanying ladies
by the Bodies of the Rite
in the Valley of Cincinnati
Steamer Island Queen

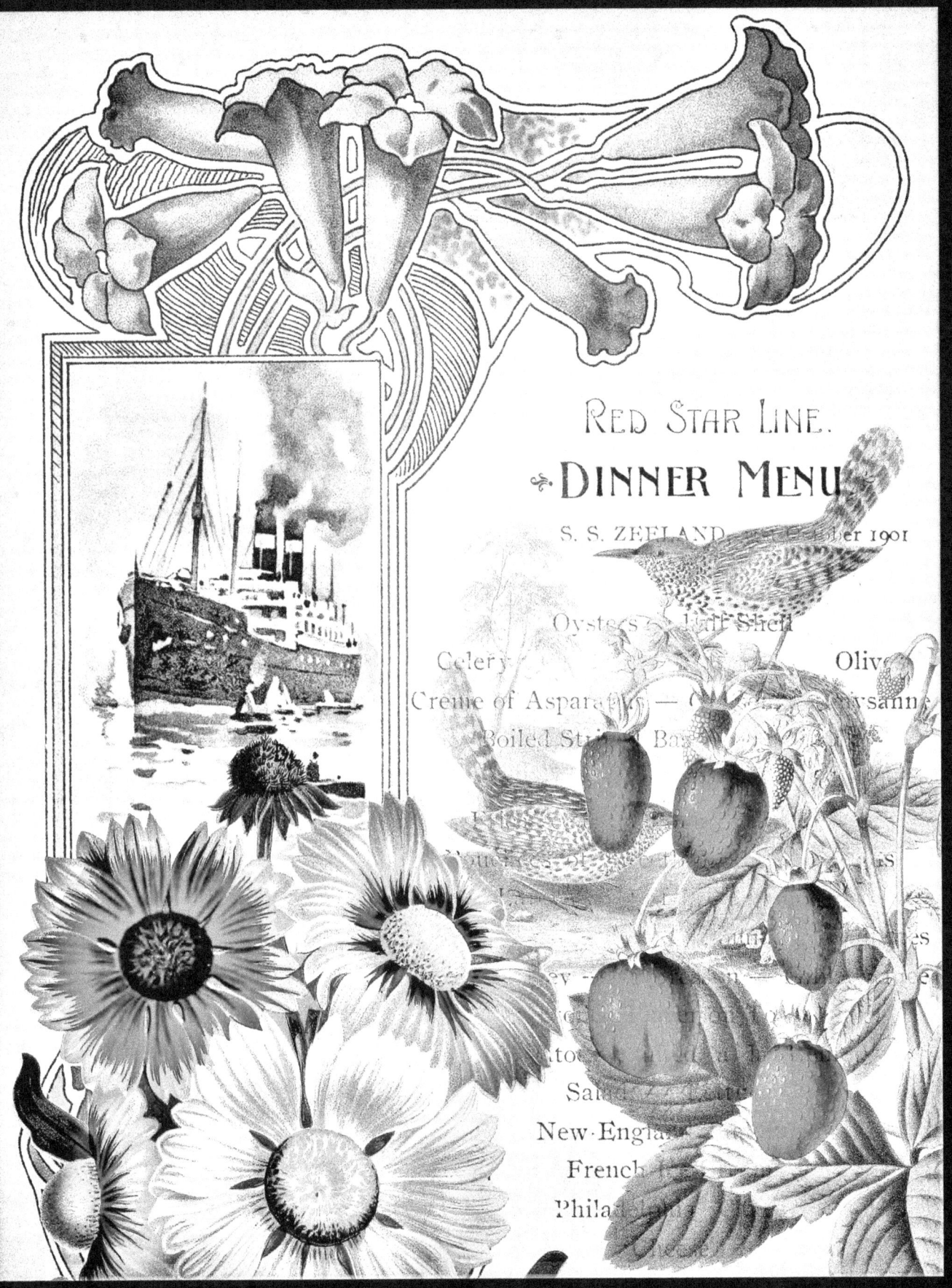

Red Star Line.
Dinner Menu
S. S. ZEELAND ... 1901

Oysters ... Shell
Celery ... Olives
Creme of Asparagus ...
Boiled Striped Bass ...

...
New England ...
French ...
Phila...

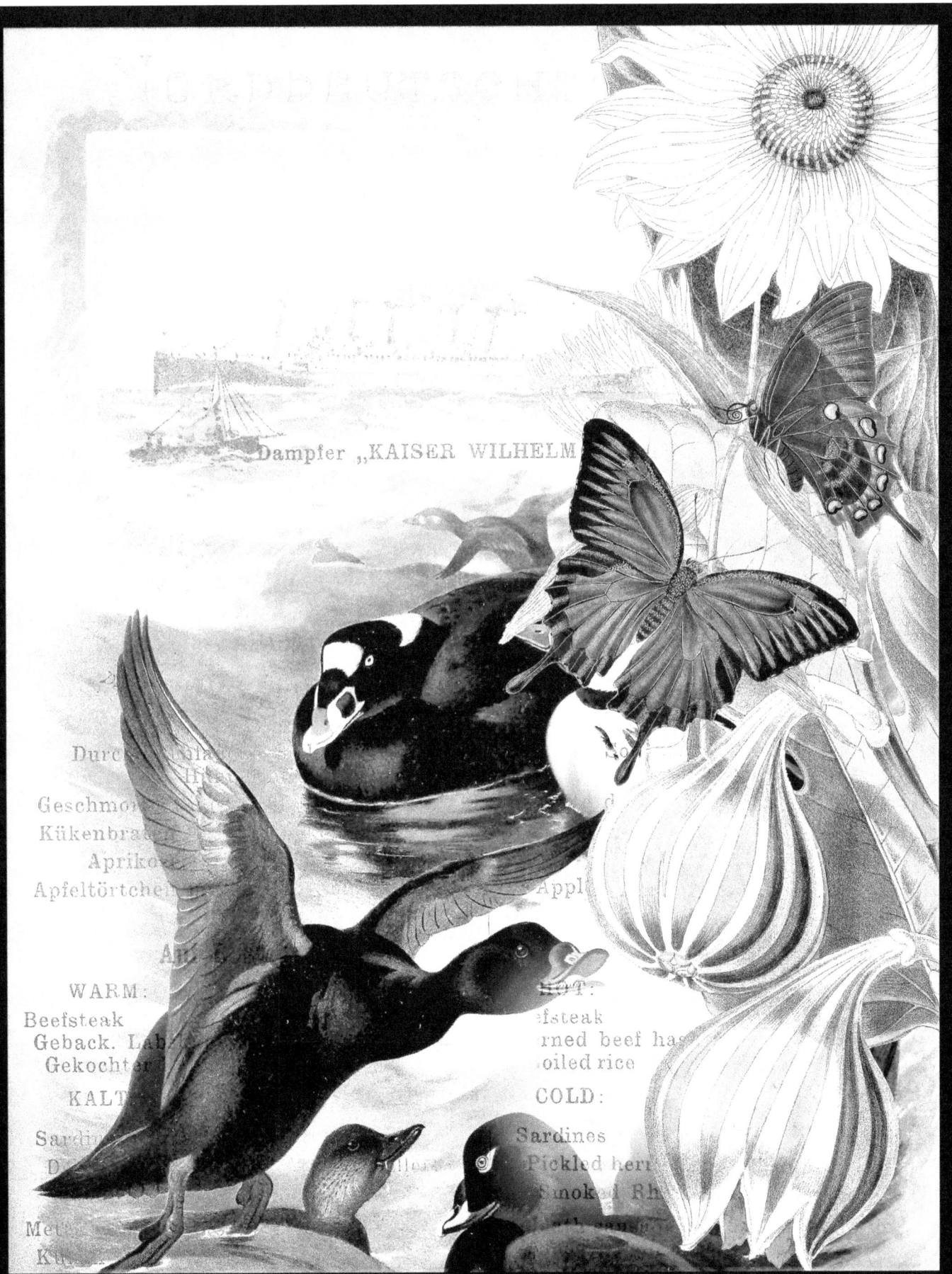

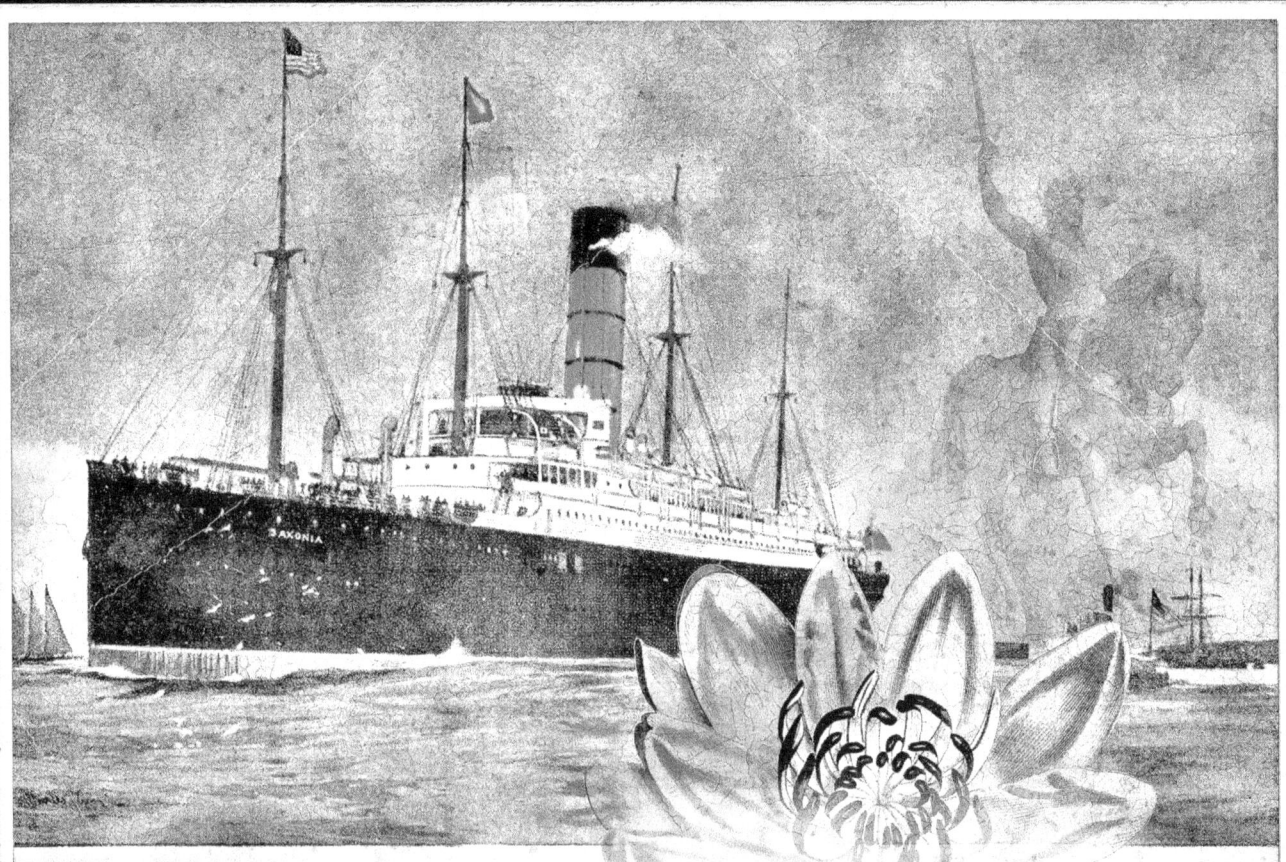

R.M.S. "ETRURIA."

Menu

Pate de foie gras   Olives Farcie   Lyon Sausage

Consomme Princesse   Potage Purre Le Grand

Halibut, Hollandaise   Spanish Mackerel, Moutarde

Grenadines de Veau, Nivernaise   Soft Shell Crabs, Americaine

Sirloin & Ribs of Beef, Pomme Croquette

Quarter of Spring Lamb, Mint Sauce

Gosling, Alsacienne   Pilau of Chicken

Cauliflowers, White Sauce   Boiled Rice   Mashed Turnips

Potatoes—New Boiled, Baked & Duchesse

Asperges en Branches

Roast Beef   Cumberland Ham   Ox Tongue

Celery

Pudding, Cream Sauce   Gooseberry Tart

Francaise   Gelee au Vin   Petit Madeleines

French Ice Cream, Wafers

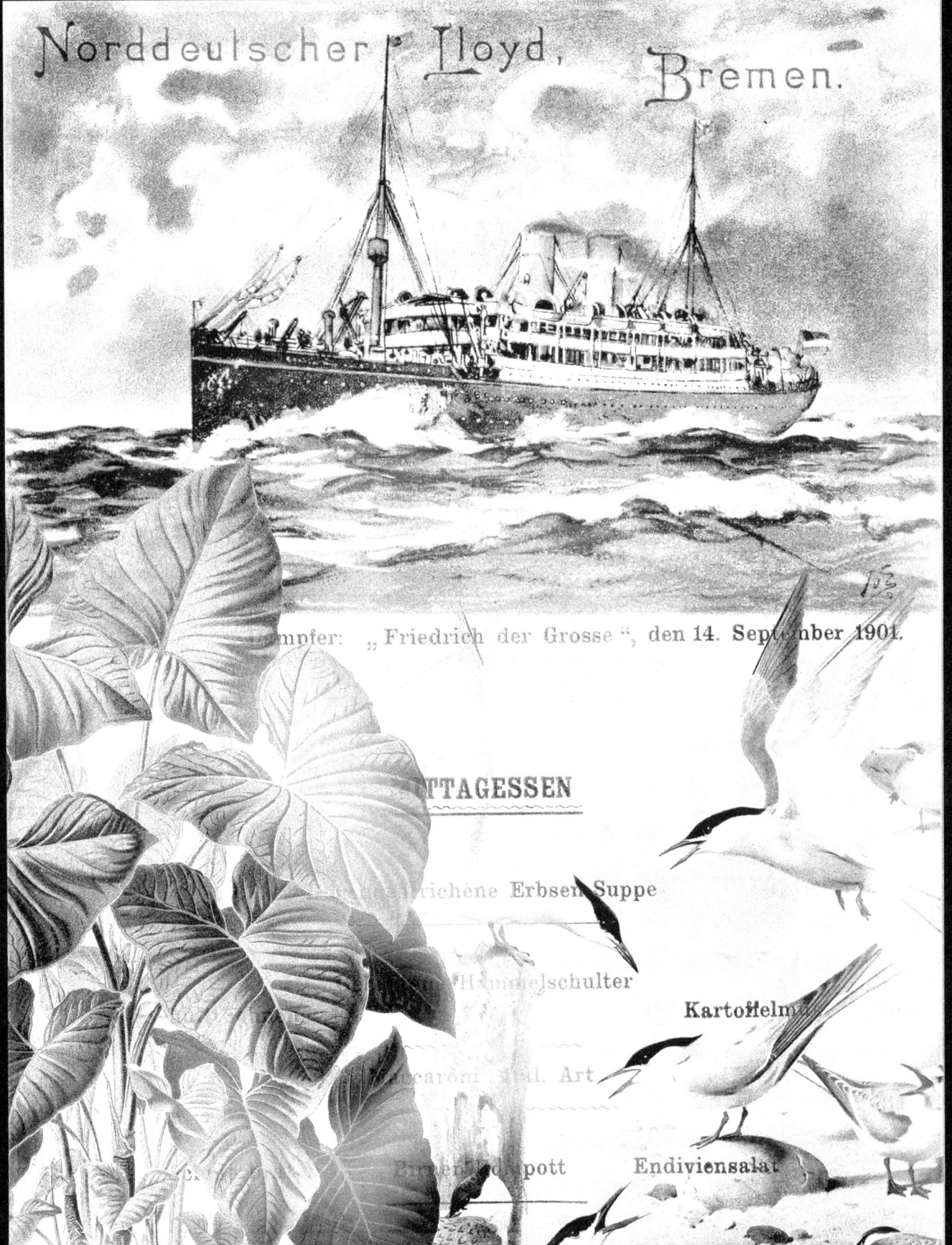

Norddeutscher Lloyd, Bremen.

Dampfer: "Friedrich der Grosse", den 14. September 1901.

MITTAGESSEN

Gestrichene Erbsen-Suppe

Hammelschulter   Kartoffeln

Macaroni ital. Art

Rinderhochrippe   Endiviensalat

NORDDEUTSCHER LLOYD
BREMEN.

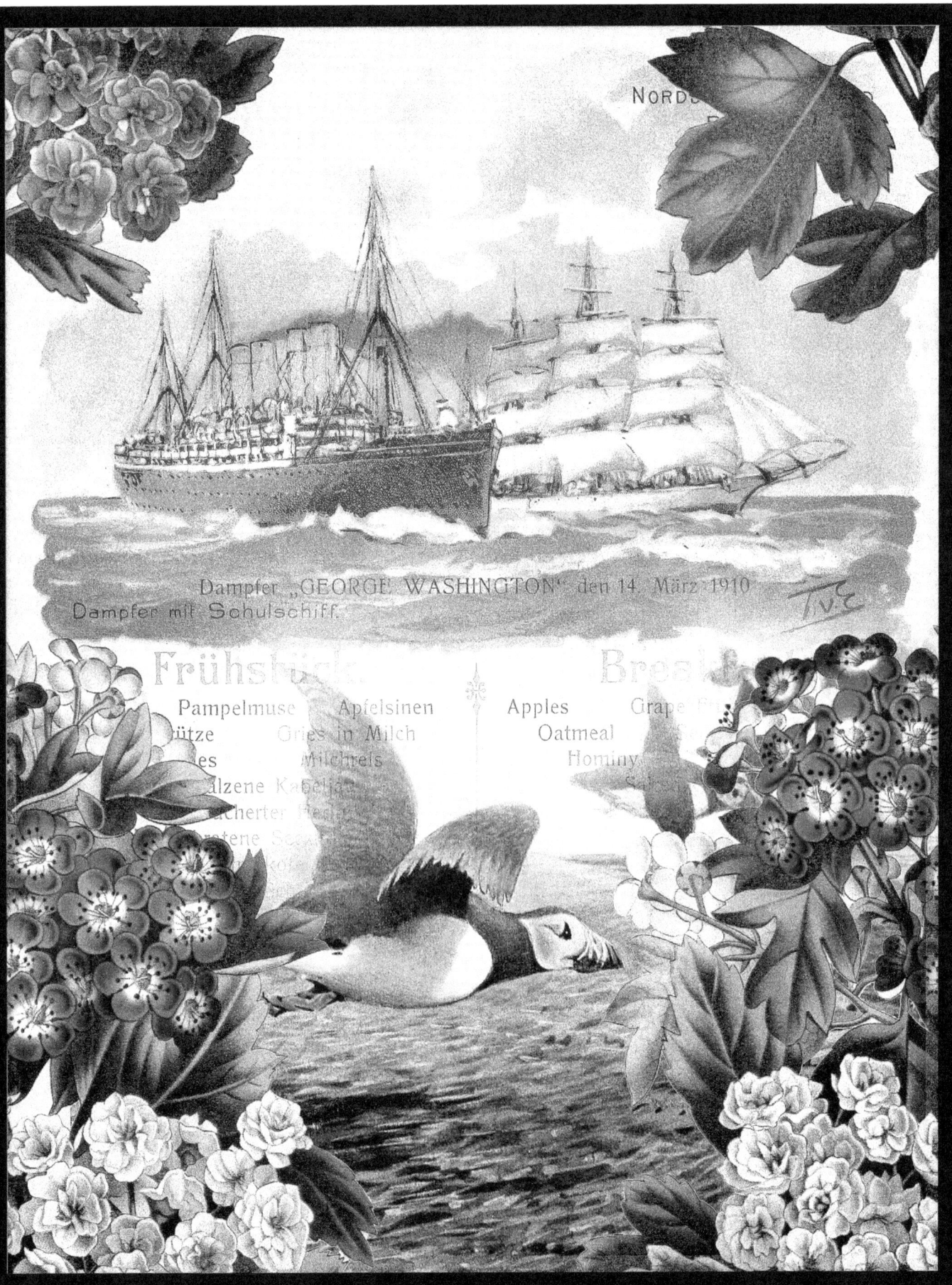

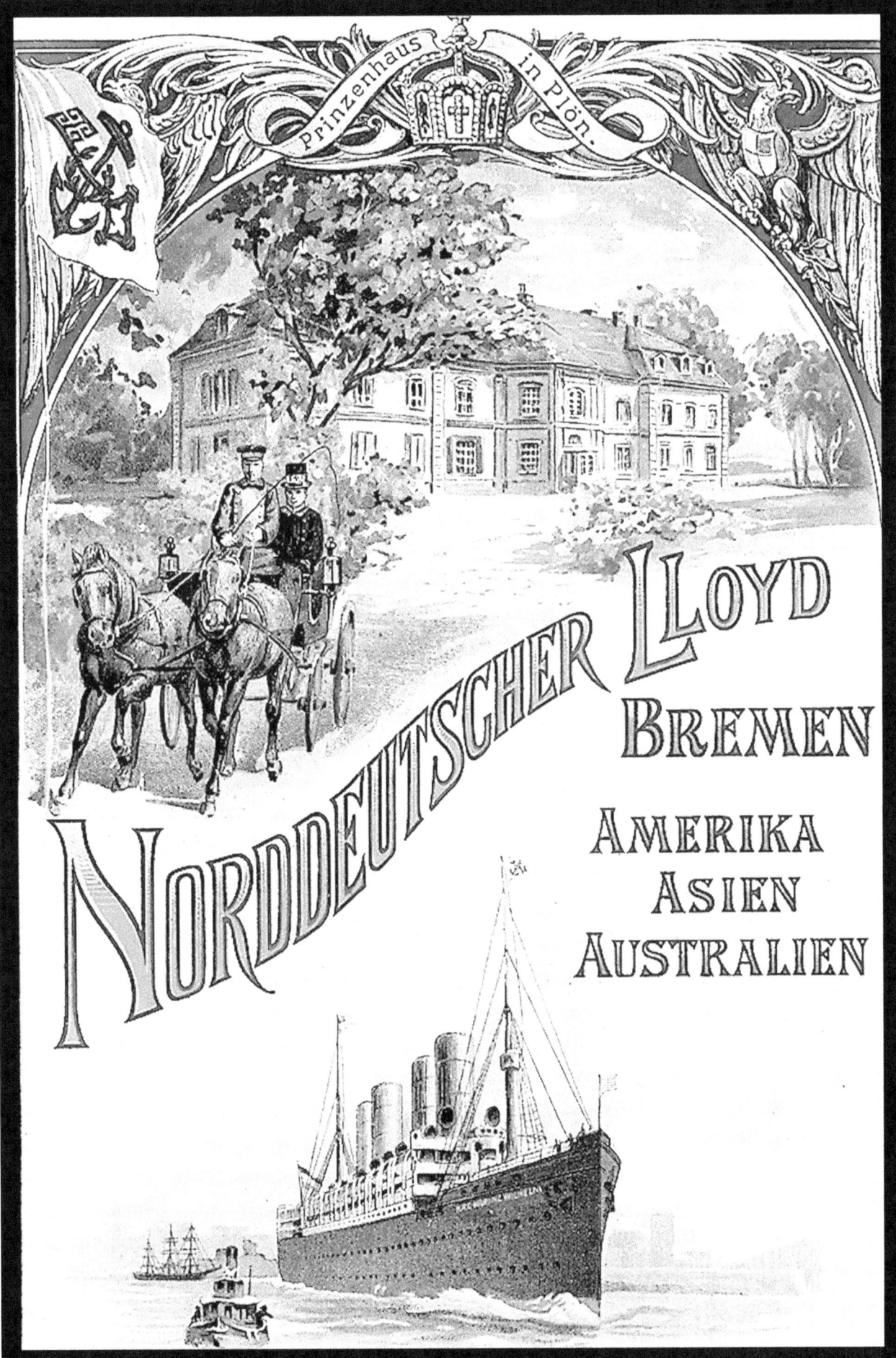

Norddeutscher Lloyd
BREMEN.

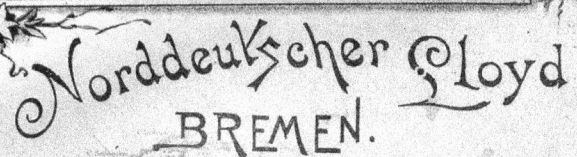

Diner: H. H. Meier den 5. Mai 1901.

Kartoffel Suppe

Hackebraten   Rosenkohl

Kalbfleisch in Curry & Reis

Kirschtörtchen

AUF BESTELLUNG:

Lachs-Mayonnaise

Caviar   Rollmops

Nagelholz   Fleischwurst

...braten

...sgurk...

... & Kartoffel Salat

Rahm Käse

NORDDEUTSCHER LLOYD
BREMEN.

ABENDampfer "GEORGE W...N" den 19. März 1910

Aepfel   Pampe...   Apfelsinen   Gr...
         ütg...   ...ies in Milch   ...neal
    Maisg...   Milchreis   ...omi...
                                          Salted M...
         Ge... ...ing   Kippe...
    Grillierter ...   S...ellfisch   ...rilled
Beefsteak, ...kotelette ... Grill   Beefsteak,...
         ...ah...chnitzel   Escalop
    Ung...sche ...albskotelette   Veal
         ...eflüge...ber sauté   Chi...
    Beefsteak m... Hindernissen   Beefsteak...
Yorkshire Schink... Wiltshire Speck   Yorkshire...
Gek...   Boiled-, Sau... Fr...
                                          Buckwh...

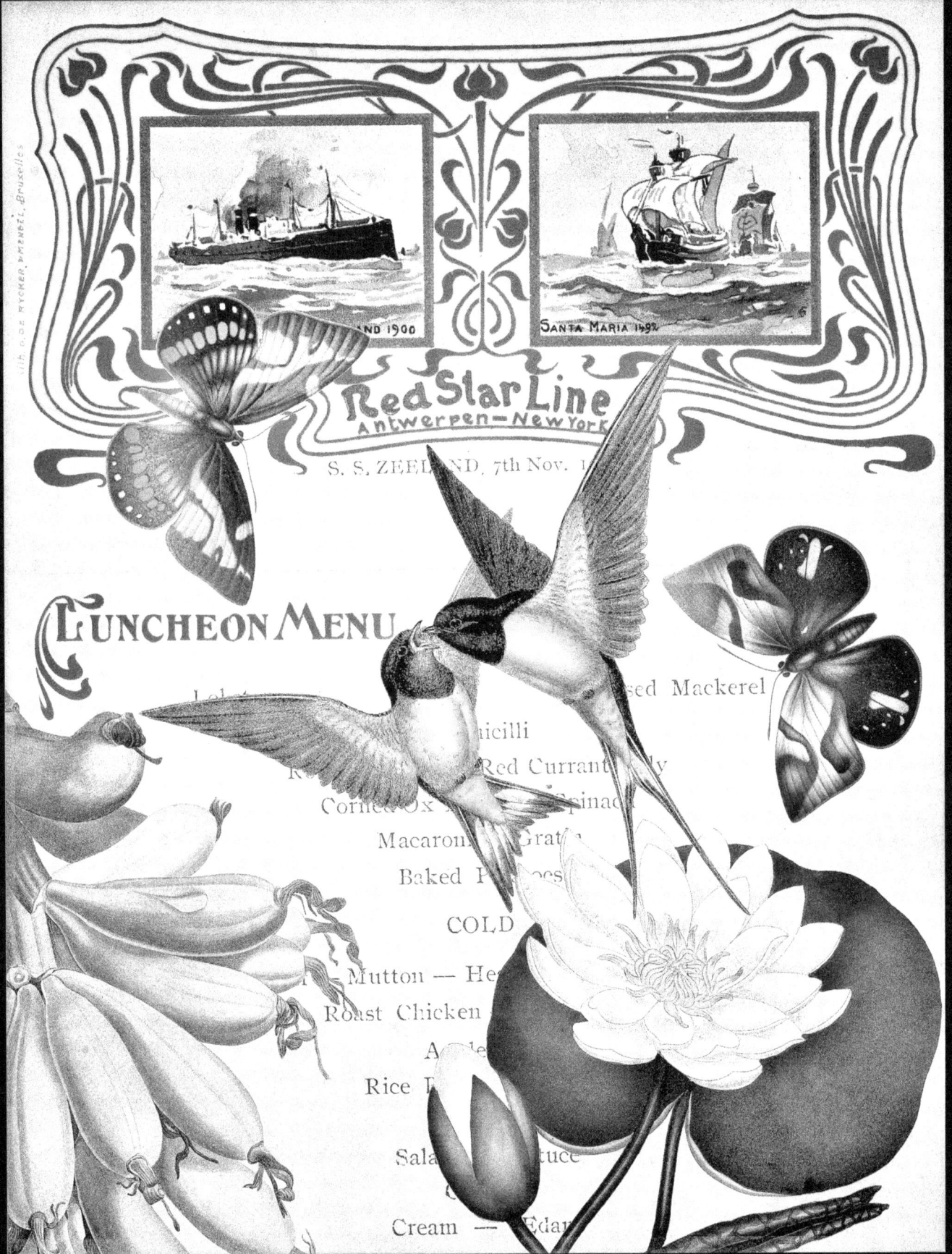

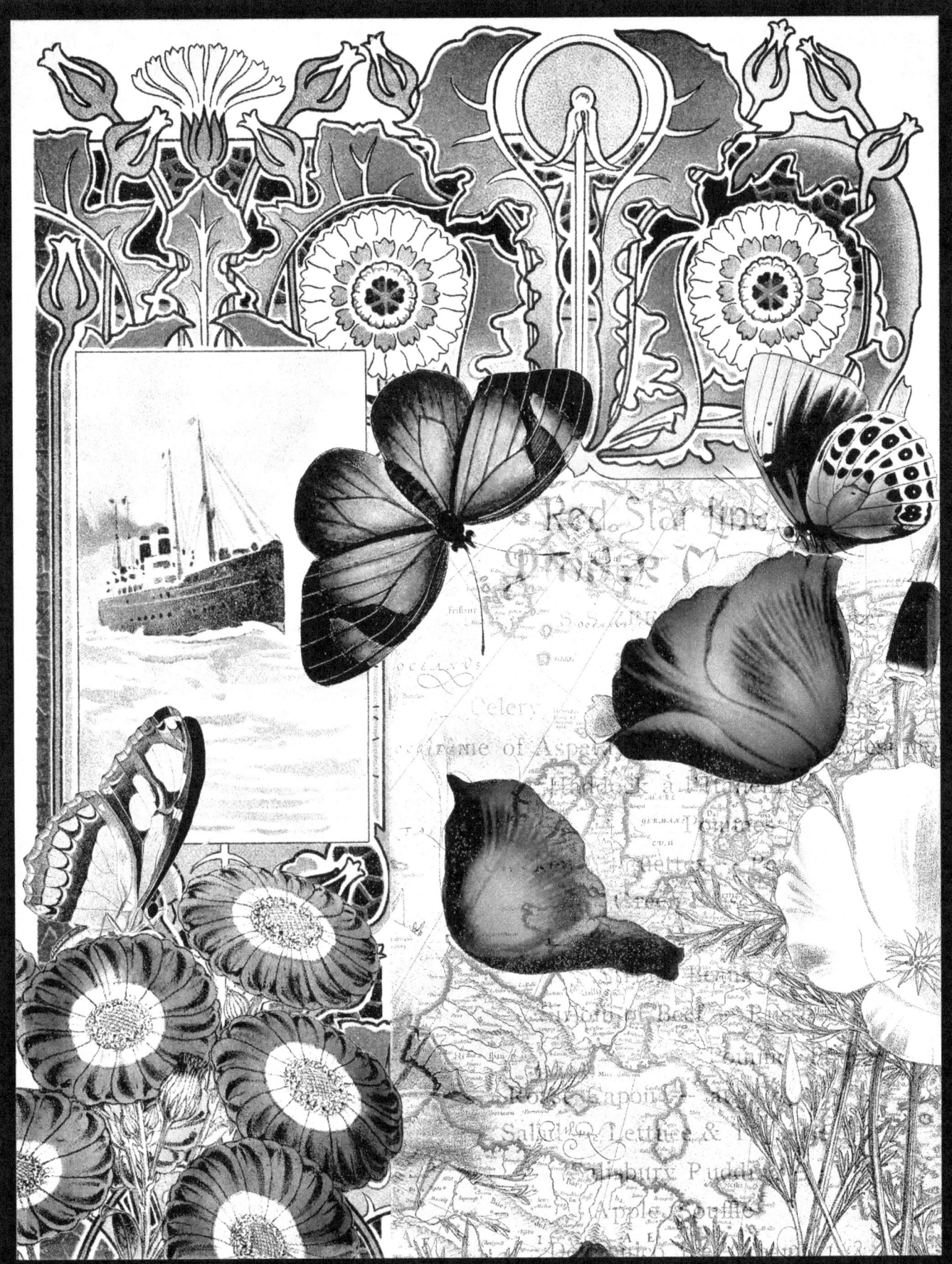

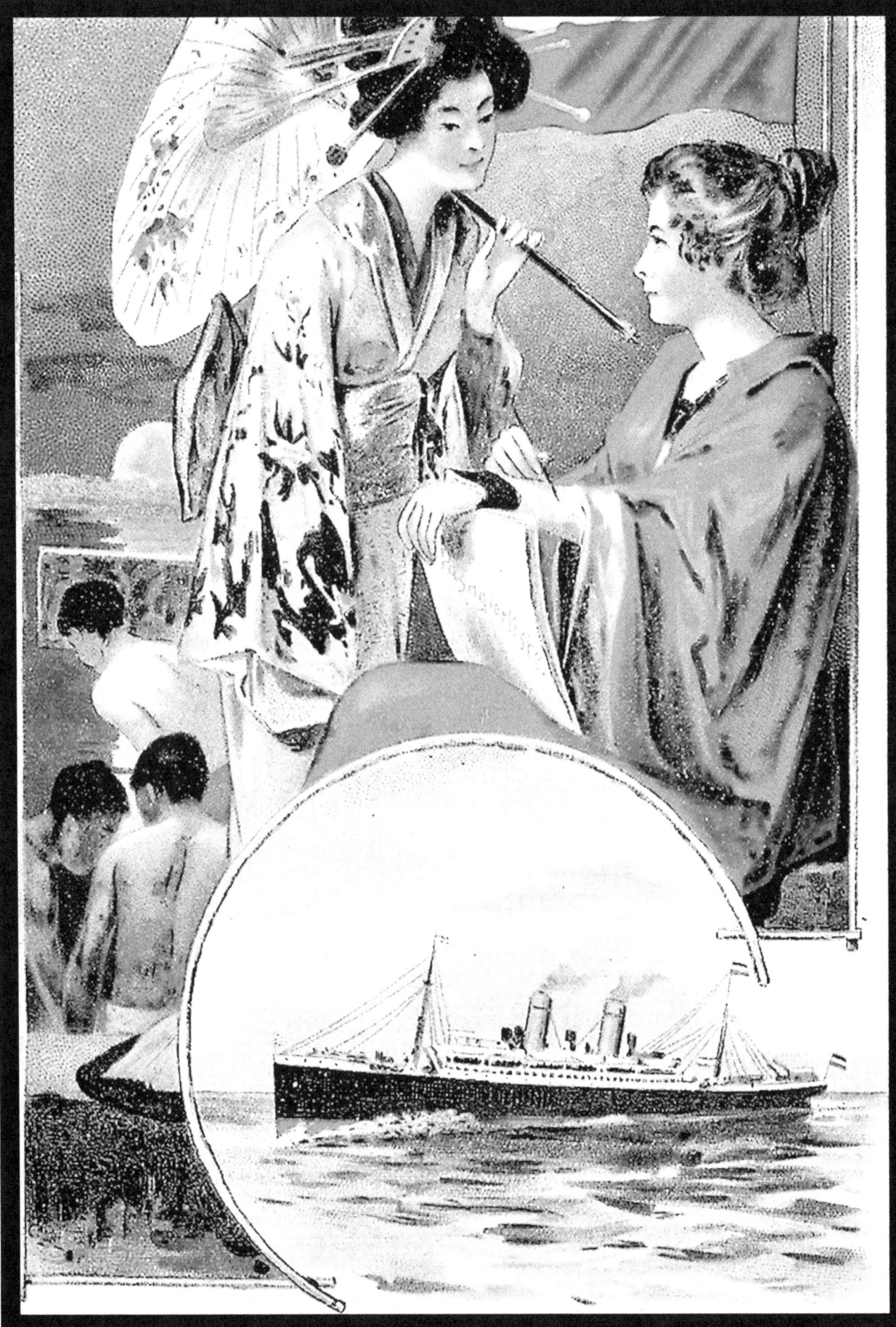

www.ingramcontent.com/pod-product-compliance
Lightning Source LLC
Chambersburg PA
CBHW080559220526
45466CB00010B/3194